1996

The Challenge of Diversity

The Challenge of Diversity

The Witness of Paul and the Gospels

David Rhoads

FORTRESS PRESS

MINNEAPOLIS

THE CHALLENGE OF DIVERSITY
The Witness of Paul and the Gospels

Many of the Scripture quotations in this book are the author's own translation.

Substantial portions of chapter 3 previously appeared in Interpretation and portions of chapter 4 in *Currents in Theology and Mission.* Used by permission.

Quotations of the letter to the Galatians in chapter 2 are from the translation of
Hans Dieter Betz in *Galatians,* Hermeneia series (Philadelphia: Fortress Press,
1979).

Scripture quotations from the New Revised Standard Version of the Bible are
copyright © 1989 by the Division of Christian Education of the National Council
of Churches of Christ in the U.S.A. and are used by permission.

Book and cover design by Joseph Bonyata

Library of Congress Cataloging-in-Publication Data

Rhoads, David M.
    The challenge of diversity : the witness of Paul and the Gospels /
by David Rhoads
        p.   cm.
    Includes bibliographical references.
    ISBN 0-8006-2982-5 (alk. paper)
    1. Bible N.T. Galatians—Criticism, interpretation, etc.
    2. Bible N.T. Gospels—Criticism, interpretation, etc.
    3. Multiculturalism—Biblical teaching. I. Title.
    BS2685.2R46 1996
    225.6—dc20   96-32292
                                                            CIP

The paper used in this publication meets the minimum requirements of the
American National Standard for Information Sciences—Permanence of Paper
for Printed Library Materials, ANSI Z329.48-1984.

Manufactured in the U.S.A.   AF 1-2982
03   02   01   3   4   5   6   7   8   9   10   11

With gratitude
For my diverse family

Sandy
Tania and Aaron
Jessica and Johnny
Anton and Natalia
Mouse

Contents

Preface

THE SEEDS FOR THIS BOOK WERE SOWN IN THE MID-1980s as a set of lectures to professional leaders in the Milwaukee Synod of the Lutheran Church in America. They were an appeal for the retention of diversity on the eve of a church merger. The long process of expanding and revising the material has led me to see more clearly the astounding diversity in the New Testament and to appreciate more fully the rich variety in contemporary Christianity. Also, since those initial lectures, I have thoroughly rethought the issue of diversity in light of the challenge of multiculturality within the church and within American society in general.

This book is addressed primarily to Christians of various denominations in the United States—to parishes, both laity and clergy, and to students. I hope the book might be useful in teaching, preaching, spiritual formation, and mission. Its aim is simply to be a source of Christian renewal at both the personal and the parish levels as together we seek to minister to one another and to the world. It is an invitation to reach beyond our own perspective and to embrace a wider circle of diverse viewpoints as legitimate expressions of the Christian life—both in the New Testament and in the contemporary church—and to be open to learn and grow from them.

Many people have given helpful responses to this manuscript in various drafts—colleagues in New Testament at the Lutheran School of Theology in Chicago, Edgar Krentz and Barbara Rossing; colleagues in the Religion Department at Carthage College, Rom Maczka, Dudley Riggle, and Dan Schowalter; along with Carol Albright, Kadi Billman, Alan Culpepper, Joanna Dewey, Inagrace Dietterich, Eleanor Doidge, Allan Hauck, Philip Hefner, Earl Hilgert, Tina Krause, Wilhelm Linss, Margaret Mitchell,

James Okoye, Mark Powell, Robert Tannehill, Sandy Roberts, Steve Samuelson, Robin Scroggs, Bill Strehlow, and Christine Thompson, among others. I am deeply grateful to them for their suggestions and their encouragement.

Produced for use with this book is a video (and audio) tape of performances of Galatians and of selections from each of the four gospels, along with a video course for parishes and a video course oriented to preaching the diversity of the Bible. These resources can be obtained from SELECT, c/o Trinity Lutheran Seminary, 2199 E. Main Street, Columbus, Ohio 43209. Telephone: (614) 235-4136.

I invite readers to respond to this book—your reactions to it (both in agreement and disagreement), your use of it, your suggestions, your personal experiences and parish experiments with diversity, along with other stories and ideas that would enrich our dialogue about renewing the church and its mission. Please write to me at: Lutheran School of Theology, 1100 E. 55th Street, Chicago, Illinois 60615. E-Mail address: drhoads@lstc.edu.

Introduction
Diversity

CHRISTIANITY TODAY MANIFESTS A WIDE VARIETY OF BELIEFS, worship patterns, organizational structures, community formations, spiritualities, ethical life-styles, and ministries to society. Christians have often viewed this variety as a liability and have grieved the fragmentation of the body of Christ. Sometimes, in an effort to eliminate the diversity, Christians have sought to convert or to marginalize other Christian sisters and brothers. When Christian groups are intolerant of one another and refuse to cooperate with one other, it is indeed a great tragedy. Diversity in itself, however, is not an aberration, nor is it a sign of brokenness. Rather, it is a great strength of the church. Diversity may be the chief reason why the Christian church has thrived through the centuries and adapted in so many parts of the world. In the future, this rich variety in Christianity may be crucial for the survival of the church and for the effectiveness of its mission. Therefore, it is important that Christians celebrate and nurture differences as a source of strength and renewal.

The present diversity in the Christian church reflects a diversity that was there from the beginning. The present multiplicity of Christian groups is not a sign of the fragmentation of the body of Christ (except when we fight with each other). Rather, it is a sign of the rich diversity that was there from the start. In the earliest beginnings of the church, there never was a pristine unity that was somehow subsequently broken. A multiplicity of Christian visions, beliefs, practices, and community formations is at the heart of the Christian faith in its origins. The early Christian movement reached out for the very purpose of creating and encompassing incredible diversity within the larger reach of God's reconciliating unity.

1

The early Christian movement meant nothing less than breaking down the dividing wall between Jews and Gentiles. And this universal vision was much more than the combining of two groups, for neither group was monolithic. On the one side, Judaism was itself multiform in that era of history—both in Palestine with its various sectarian groups and among the communities of Jews dispersed throughout the Roman Empire and throughout the Parthian Empire to the east. On the other side, there was the multiplicity of Gentile nations. The Greek word *Gentiles* literally means "nations." Across the ancient Mediterranean world, there was an incredible array of local ethnic communities, subcultures, and language groups within the aegis of the Roman Empire. That is, there were many "nations" within Northern Africa and the south; Palestine and the east; Asia Minor, Greece, and the north; Italy and the west; and on the islands in the Mediterranean Sea. The region around the Mediterranean Sea was multilingual, multiracial, and multiethnic, with many different religions and philosophies. These Jewish groups and Gentile nations comprised the multiplicity of cultures that Christianity sought to address and to embrace. In this multicultural arena, the diversity of early Christianity took shape.

The earliest Christian movements proclaimed the idea that "community" was not to be based on uniformity but would cut across different social and cultural locations and embrace people very different from each other. Jesus proclaimed a vision of life in the future kingdom in which people would come from east and west, north and south, to sit at the banquet table together. In different ways, the New Testament writers believed that the one creator was now providing the reconciliation that enabled early followers of Jesus eagerly to reach the diverse humanity of all creation. Early Christian communities challenged and empowered people to live by the values that would make such universalism possible—the love of enemy, the commitment to reconciliation, the refusal to dominate, the willingness to forgive, the eagerness to value the gifts of others, the offer of unconditional love, and so on. Such values fostered great variety in the shape and composition of early communities.

With regard to the particular writings that comprise the New Testament collection, individual writers strove to embrace diverse

Jewish groups and Gentile nations in a number of ways. Matthew depicts Jesus sending the disciples to "make disciples of all nations" (Matthew 28:19). Luke foreshadows great diversity in the church when he lists people from all over the world in Jerusalem for Pentecost who hear the disciples praising God in their own languages—Parthians, Medes, Elamites, Mesopotamians, Judeans, Cappadocians, people from Pontus, Asia Minor, Phrygia, Pamphylia, and Libya, along with Romans, Cretans, and Arabs (Acts 2:5–11). In his letters, Paul, the Apostle to the Gentiles, proclaims the gospel in divergent theological ways appropriate to the distinct cultural context of each audience he addressed—Galatians in central Asia Minor, Philippians as a Roman colony, Thessalonians of Macedonia, Corinthians of Achaia, and the Roman Christians. The book of Revelation claims that Jesus has drawn followers from "every tribe and language and people and nation" (5:9). Each of these biblical visions of expansive inclusivity preserved the particularity and distinctiveness of the different cultural groups as they became part of the wider Christian movement.

As a collection, the New Testament writings themselves witness to the significantly different visions of life and diverse theological beliefs that were forged out in this period. The New Testament includes vastly divergent manifestations of the Christian life—diverse theological beliefs, practices, rituals, community structures, ethical guidelines, and ethnic identities. The diverse writings of the New Testament are only the tip of an iceberg of diversity among traditions in early Christianity. The writings of the New Testament are merely representative of a much greater diversity in the scattered communities of the early Christian movement. Diversity is fundamental to the biblical witness. The later Christians who decided which writings to include in the Christian canon were well aware of the differences among the books they selected.[1] Instead of choosing only those books that agreed with one theology and church order, they chose the writings closest to Jesus in time and influence, and they allowed the pluralism to stand. By including such variety, they chose wisely—for their own day as well as for ours. Diversity in the New Testament is not, therefore, a cause for concern but a reason for rejoicing. God has provided for such diversity in the New Testament, and we need it for our life together.

The foundational importance of diversity in Christianity is reinforced by the recognition that diversity is an indispensible part of life, indeed a crucial dimension of the way in which God works in the world. If we step back from thinking about the church for a moment and reflect on a larger "theology of diversity," we realize that diversity is integral to God's ongoing creation of the world. God created diversity. Through Christ, God redeems diversity. As creatures, we need a diversity of plants and animals in order to survive on this planet. We need a diversity of cultures and peoples to have a healthy humanity that will be adaptable for the future. We need diversity not only to perpetuate life but also to thrive and to enrich our lives together. In the same way, our Christian communities need to be diverse in the wealthiest kind of way. For in our Christian witness today, we need to embrace diversity and learn to relish it or we may be going against the very grain of God's creative presence among us.

The plain witness of creation is that God delights in diversity. God works through diversity in all of creation. Life on earth would be quickly jeopardized if we lost a large number of wheat strains or species of beetles. We humans too often fail to realize how much we depend for our existence on the variety of flora and fauna that enable life to be adaptable and flexible amid varied and changing conditions. The capacity for life to thrive on our planet depends upon a rich variety of plant strains and animal species. We have been learning that hard lesson from the present ecological crises as whole species of plant and animal life have been disappearing at an alarming rate due to the destruction of rain forests and other ecosystems. It is crucial for us to preserve every species of flora and fauna along with the ecosystems that support them. God created such biological diversity, and we are called to cherish it.

In a similar way, we are more and more aware in our own time of the importance of human diversity throughout the world and of the increasing multiplicity of ethnic and cultural traditions now residing in the United States. The United States has always been made up of many cultures. Yet the extent and nature of the mix is now more complex than ever. Quite simply, America has come to encompass the races and cultures of the world. When multiculturalism recently arose as a popular concept, it initially referred to the ascendancy of cultures other than the dominant culture. However, no longer does multiculturality refer to "those cultures other than the dominant culture." The dominant European-American cultures are now becoming relativized, and many cultures are gaining a greater stake in the process. Multiculturality is now a matter of "interculturality," groups relating together in mutual interdependence. It takes a mental shift to redefine America in this new way, to see that what we most share together now as Americans is the common experience of interculturality itself.

This situation recalls the great American melting pot of diverse peoples from Europe, of the people brought here forcibly from various places in Africa who built and shaped the United States, and of the destruction or coerced assimilation of Native Americans. As time passed, many families have forgotten their origins and simply think of themselves as "Americans," without an awareness of the roots that have shaped and continue to shape them. Now, however, there is concern not to lose discrete cultural identities in a melting pot of assimilation into the dominant culture. There is a desire to preserve and to reclaim distinct ethnic traditions, languages, and worldviews as part of our life together. The recovery of Native American languages, beliefs, and practices is one example of this present desire that no cultural heritage be lost. African American men and women are also actively seeking to recover the roots of their rich history and traditions. Instead of a melting pot, we now imagine our common life together as a quilt or a kaleidoscope or a mosaic of distinct pieces that together create a design greater than its parts.

Recovering and protecting our cultural diversity is a crucial part of our life together as people in this nation and on this planet. Could it be that our survival on the planet requires preserving a variety of cultural traditions, social groupings, and lifestyles? Are we not challenged to preserve a rich diversity of sociocultural forms along with the ecosystems that support them, just as we seek to preserve a diversity of biological species and the ecosystems that support them?

What is the situation of the churches in the midst of this cultural diversity? All religious expressions, of course, are also at the same time cultural expressions. As such, churches in the United States have shared the cultural diversity of the country. However, most denominations have been associated in background and composition with one or two ethnic groups. Similarly, most ethnic communities in this country have been associated with one or two denominations. For example, people from Scandinavian countries were primarily Lutheran, people with English heritage were primarily Episcopalian or Methodist, and Hispanic Americans were predominantly Roman Catholic and Pentecostal.

Now, however, the whole scene is changing, for churches in the United States are experiencing ethnic and racial diversity in new ways. Today, there are Hispanic American Methodist Churches, Korean American Presbyterian Churches, Japanese American Lutheran Churches, and so on. Churches are experiencing greater pluralism in denominations as a whole and within individual parishes. Many parishes have significant representation of several ethnic communities. Some congregations are coordinating the cooperative ministries of several communities composed of different nationalities and languages within the same building. There is today an incredible mixture of ethnic and religious traditions. That is why it is so important today to treat religion in the United States in terms of the rich diversity of cultural, ethnic, and racial groups within and across denominations.

Such diversity in the nation and in the church and in our daily lives is often frightening to us, despite our deep longing for the ties that bind us across differences. We are often uncomfortable with ambiguity and difference, preferring to be with "people like ourselves." Unfortunately, our churches themselves often reflect our avoidance of diversity, because they are so frequently made up of people of the same social group. In our daily lives, we relate to people different from ourselves, but often in very limited roles. Many of us do not really know people very well who are different in economic level or educational difference or racial identity or language or political allegiance or religious affiliation—unless they are people whom we have had to figure out in order to survive! Our fear and avoidance of difference is fueled by the intractable religious and cultural wars throughout the world and the volatile ethnic conflicts that have flared up in our own country. We tend to have limited tolerance for diversity, perhaps because we fear that we may find no common ground with others and that unpleasant and harmful conflicts will be inevitable. We

fear disruption or loss or assimilation or erosion of our own religious and cultural particularity.

But what if we faced up to our avoidance and began by honor-
ing differences? What if we dared to take difference rather than
conformity as the fundamental starting point for relationships?
What if we faced our discomfort with ambiguity and chose to
value diversity as the indispensable basis for mutual interdependence together? What if we discovered our unity through the
courage to explore our differences? Our instincts may tell us to be
cautious. Yet, following our instincts without reflection can be as
dangerous as ignoring our instincts. Besides, Jesus proposed that
our common salvation involves acting in spite of our instincts,
such as loving our enemies or losing our lives for others rather
than saving our lives. What if, like the early Christians, we
assumed that there is no common ground for unity within human
beings themselves and that God alone is the reality who unites
us? In this way, we might discover that respecting and embracing
differences among all people under God's creation is in fact the
path to discovering and embracing the full measure of God's
unity. True, we need to be savvy about points of view and beliefs
that are destructive and dehumanizing. But we need to do that
out of a fundamental commitment to the inherent value of diversity in God's larger embrace—and with a willingness to take risks.

For centuries, churches have struggled with the issue of unity
by means of ecumenical discussions between denominations.
Sometimes these conversations have led to conflicts between
vying points of doctrine. The conflicts have sometimes resulted in
silence, following the familiar admonition never to discuss politics
or religion. Yet we are in a new day where we can hold dialogues
in respect and appreciation for the differences among denominations without assuming one is right and the other wrong. We recognize the value and validity of a diversity of legitimate points of
view from which we can all learn and be enriched. We now realize
that the different contemporary expressions of Christianity are, for
the most part, equally rooted in different parts of the New Testament! The greater awareness of cultural diversity is enhancing our
appreciation for the diverse traditions in the New Testament to
which different groups appeal for inspiration and support.

This new diversity within denominations is providing challenges to churches as never before. How might the church look in this new intercultural situation? How might we re-vision our life together? How might we envision the realm of God in the world in which we live? How might various cultural groups relate to each other within denominations and across denominational lines? How might we find resources in the diversity in the New Testament to enable us to deal with our situation?

Our churches have an opportunity now to embrace and foster diversity in a new way—a way that honors difference and does not require people to give up their cultural identity in order to participate in a particular denomination. Cultural diversity within church bodies and local congregations is an essential dimension of life together in Christ. Faithfulness to the Bible calls for it, and diversity is a sign of the work of the Spirit. As such, we are called to become intentional communities of diversity. Anyone who enters a worship service and sees people from many different ethnic groups and social locations experiences the strength and universality of the gospel. Such diversity gives the church durability and adaptability. Diversity enables the church to meet the needs of many different people, to address and embrace the cultural distinctiveness of various ethnic groups, to adapt to changing times and circumstances, to ensure that Christian life remains fresh and vital, and to enable us to be more imaginative in the church's mission to the world. God created such religious diversity, and we will surely need it to carry out our ministry in the world.

Appreciating the diversity in the New Testament is one way to foster such renewal for the church. As we have said, early Christianity arose in the mix and midst of a cultural pluralism even greater than the pluralism we now experience. The earliest multiform expressions of Christianity forged out in the pluralistic world of the first century parallel the cultural and theological diversity we experience in the church today. Learning from the pluralism in the New Testament can be crucial for strengthening the pluralistic mission and ministry of the church. If we Christians want to bear the full testimony of the New Testament to the world today, it will take the diverse witness of all of us. Furthermore, we can learn from the New Testament writers about love and unconditional acceptance and reconciliation and mutuality in community. If we Christians knew how to deal with diversity in the profound ways offered by the New Testament, we could be at the cutting edge of bringing reconciliation to a fractured world today.

The first step in this venture might be an openness to the diversity at the core of our faith. As we experience the challenge of differing biblical witnesses, we open ourselves to crucial resources for renewal. Here are two examples that illustrate the possibilities for such a renewal of the church from the diversity in the New Testament.

> Example one: Some years ago, Father Raymond Brown, a Roman Catholic scholar who taught at Union Theological Seminary in New York, told the story of what happened when the Roman Catholic churches changed the lectionary readings. Roman Catholics were accustomed every year to hearing the Matthean version of Peter's confession of Jesus as the Messiah, after which Jesus praises him, calls Peter a "Rock," and declares that he will build his church on that rock. Matthew uses this story to root the founding of the church in the ministry of Jesus, a passage crucial for the self-identity of Roman Catholics. In the new lectionary, however, there began a three-year cycle in which passages from Matthew appear during only one of the three years. In other years of the lectionary, the readings originate primarily from Mark and Luke. In the second year of the new lectionary, Roman Catholic churches heard the story of Peter's confession as it appears in the Gospel of Mark. In Mark's version, Jesus responds to Peter's confession by rebuking Peter and the other disciples to be quiet about it, and then he immediately announces his impending suffering and death, whereupon Peter rebukes Jesus and Jesus in turn rebukes Peter. Mark's version has no founding of the church, but rather prepares Christians to suffer for the good news. Father Brown recounts how in parish after parish people came up to the priests after service with shocked faces and asked what happened to the part about the "rock" and the church!

Father Brown's story shows how Christian communities tend to assume that the whole New Testament says only what they themselves believe or practice. His point was that Christians can learn from other parts of the New Testament—other theologies, other practices, other experiences, other ways of being Christian. Also, in studying these biblical traditions, we can learn about each other, because communities that differ in cultural and denominational makeup draw upon differing biblical traditions for their faith and life.

Example two: A seminary professor recently invited each member of her class on Cross-Cultural Preaching to bring to class the one line from the Bible that meant the most to them, the one they would most like to preach on. The students in the class were African American, Hispanic American, Native American, Asian American, and European American men and women of different ages who represented a variety of ecclesiastical traditions and social backgrounds. The result was a rich variety of passages, among them: "Let justice roll down like waters and righteousness like a mighty stream" (Amos); "Though I walk through the darkest valley, I fear no evil, for you are with me" (Psalm 23); "The kingdom of God has arrived; repent and have faith in the good news" (Mark); "You must be reborn" (John); "In Christ, there is neither Jew nor Greek, neither slave nor free, no male and female" (Paul); "Love your enemies" (Matthew); "Religion that is pure and undefiled before God is this: To care for orphans and widows in their distress and to keep oneself unstained by the world" (James); "For by grace you have been saved through faith: and this is not your own doing, it is a gift of God" (Ephesians); "But you are a chosen race, a royal priesthood, a holy nation, God's own people, in order that you may proclaim the mighty acts of him who called you out of darkness into his marvelous light" (1 Peter); "There is no fear in love, but perfect love casts out fear" (1 John); "They have conquered him by the blood of the lamb and by the word of their testimony, for they did not cling to life even in the face of death" (Revelation). In the class, all students explained why their passage was so important to them.

Then the teacher asked the students to exchange their biblical passages with each other. She assigned the students to preach on the verse each had now received, after studying the passage in its biblical context and with sensitivity to the cultural context of the student who had initially offered the passage. Through the process of the class, the students came to appreciate the diversity in the Bible. They also broadened and deepened their understanding of Christian faith and vocation by grappling with passages that other contemporary Christians from different social locations found so important for their faith. These students now had greater resources to minister in a variety of circumstances and were much better prepared to serve the whole church and to lead the church in serving the whole world.

The diversity evident in this seminary class of North Americans can be multiplied in relation to Christians throughout the world. Christians in Latin America tend to draw upon biblical depictions of the kingdom of God as the means to announce good news to the poor. Many Asian Christians develop the motif of the pain-love of God in Jesus for suffering humanity, in response to which we are to become suffering servants who liberate others for a greater sense of humanity. Some Black African Christians emphasize liberation from socioeconomic oppression through an active struggle involving redemptive suffering, as Jesus demonstrated in his life and death. Also, women and men in each culture often draw upon differing biblical traditions and themes that are distinctive to their concerns and struggles. We have so much to learn from each other as Christians and from the differences of the biblical witnesses upon which our various traditions depend. The possibilities for renewal seem endless.

Thus, attending to the diversity in the Bible can be a rich source of renewal for the church today. Diversity in the Bible is a rich celebration of the complexities of the human condition and of the manifestations of God in our midst. The multiplicity of belief and practice in the New Testament promotes openness and leads us to welcome others who are different and to learn from them. The diversity in the canon undercuts the human tendency to claim absolute truth for any one Christian belief system. It stands against intolerance and urges us to depend on each other for a full witness to the truth of God. It is a call to respect and celebrate diversity in the church and in the world as an expression of God's love of diversity in creation.

This book addresses Christian individuals and communities in the hope that experiencing the diversity in the New Testament will help to revitalize the church. The approach of the book is to look at a few representative writings of the New Testament as a way to illustrate the diversity in early Christianity. The emphasis on diversity in this study is not meant to suggest that any diversity at all is a good thing, nor is it meant to foster the kind of relativism that says any opinion or belief is as good as any other. We are limiting ourselves to a study of diversity evident in the New Testament; and we do so in the hope of fostering a deep appreciation for the indispensability of diversity in the church and in life as a whole. In so doing, we seek to stimulate the kind of dialogue, sharing, and differences of opinion from which we can all grow together. If in some fundamental way we can together learn to relish, indeed, to create genuine diversity within the church, perhaps we can also be a source of healing in the conflicts and struggles of our pluralistic society.

The first chapter of this book will suggest ways we can read the New Testament to discern and appreciate its differing visions of life. Following this, the chapters that comprise the heart of the book will look at five different New Testament writings—the letter to the Galatians and each of the four Gospels, which together illustrate the diversity in the New Testament. The last chapter will offer some ways in which New Testament diversity might engender renewal in personal and communal life.

This book is about diversity in the New Testament and its implications for contemporary Christianity. The focus on diversity here is not meant to diminish in any way the equally important concept of unity. Unity and diversity belong together, even though we are not giving equal space to them. In an epilogue, we will reflect briefly on ways in which we might talk about unity without compromising diversity.

Note

1. The word *canon* refers to the collection of writings regarded as scripture. The canon of the Western church was finalized in the fifth century. Some writings considered to be scripture by some groups were not included, in some cases because of theological concerns, but mostly because they were not thought to be written by one of the twelve apostles or someone close to an apostle. See *The Formation of the Christian Biblical Canon,* by Lee McDonald.

Further Reading

Anderson, Gerald and Thomas Stransky, editors. *Christ's Lordship and Religious Pluralism.* Maryknoll: Orbis, 1981.

Buenker, John and Lorman Ratner, editors. *Multiculturalism in the United States: A Comparative Guide to Acculturation and Ethnicity.* New York: Greenwood, 1992.

Davidson, Art. *Endangered Peoples.* San Francisco: Sierra Club Books, 1993.

Elizondo, Virgilio. *The Future Is Mestizo: Where Life and Cultures Meet.* Bloomington: Meyer Stone, 1988.

Felder, Cain Hope, editor. *Stony the Road We Trod: African-American Biblical Interpretation.* Minneapolis: Fortress, 1991.

Fitzpatrick, Joseph. *One Church, Many Cultures: The Challenge of Diversity*. Kansas City: Sheed and Ward, 1987.

Goldberg, David Theo, editor. *Multiculturalism: A Critical Reader*. Oxford: Blackwell, 1994.

Gonzalez, Justo. *Out of Every Tribe and Nation: Christian Theology at the Ethnic Roundtable*. Nashville: Abingdon, 1992.

Grant, Jackie. *White Woman's Christ and Black Woman's Jesus: Feminist Christology and Womanist Response*. Atlanta: Scholars Press, 1989.

King, Ursala, editor. *Feminist Theology from the Third World*. Maryknoll: Orbis, 1994.

Kyung, Chung Hyun. *The Struggle to be the Sun Again: Introducing Asian Women's Theology*. Maryknoll: Orbis, 1990.

Lewontin, Richard. *Human Diversity*. New York: W. H. Freeman, 1982.

McDonald, Lee. *The Formation of the Christian Biblical Canon*, revised edition. Peabody, Mass.: Hendrickson, 1995.

Mann, Charles and Mark Plummer. *Noah's Choice: The Future of Endangered Species*. New York: Knopf, 1995.

Mosala, Itumeleng. *Biblical Hermeneutics and Black Theology in South Africa*. Grand Rapids: Eerdmans, 1989.

Pope-Levison, Priscilla and John Levison. *Jesus in Global Contexts*. Louisville: Westminster/John Knox, 1992.

Royal, Robert, editor. *Reinventing the American People: Unity and Diversity Today*. Grand Rapids: Eerdmans, 1995.

Sample, Tex. *U.S. Lifestyles and Mainline Churches*. Louisville: Westminster/John Knox, 1990.

Schlesinger, Arthur. *The Disuniting of America*. New York: W. W. Norton, 1992.

Sugirtharajah, R. S., editor. *Voices from the Margin: Interpreting the Bible in the Third World*. London: SPCK, 1991.

Takaki, Ronald. *A Different Mirror: A History of Multicultural America*. Boston: Little, Brown, and Company, 1993.

Tamez, Elsa, editor. *Through Her Eyes: Women's Theology from Latin America*. Maryknoll: Orbis, 1989.

Taylor, Charles. *Multiculturalism*. Princeton: Princeton University Press, 1994.

Troeger, Thomas. *The Parable of Ten Preachers*. Nashville: Abingdon, 1992.

Walzer, Michael. *Spheres of Justice: A Defense of Pluralism and Equality*. New York: Basic Books, 1983.

Wilson, Edward O. *The Diversity of Life*. Cambridge: Harvard University Press, 1992.

1
Reading for Diversity

WE CAN GAIN RENEWAL FOR THE CHURCH by the study and proclamation of the different writings of the New Testament because different biblical traditions introduce us to fresh ways of considering the Christian walk, new ways to imagine being Christian. Until we experience the diversity in the New Testament, we will not fully appreciate either the challenge or the renewal possible from the biblical writings. What we say here applies equally well to the whole Bible, even though our focus will be on the New Testament.

Diversity in the New Testament

The New Testament is not one book. It is a collection of writings. The authors differ in their views of the human condition, in their understandings of the Christian life, and in their articulations of the work of Jesus as the Christ. Although the Gospels, especially the first three, have many similarities, they also have striking differences in their portraits of Jesus and their depictions of the Christian life. Paul's letters contain differing theologies because they were addressed to different churches. The catholic epistles—Hebrews, James, 1 and 2 Peter, Jude, and the letters of John—each have distinctive Christian perspectives. Needless to say, the book of Revelation is in a class by itself. For the most part, these writings were not general tracts addressed to a broad audience; rather, each writing emerged from a particular community and addressed a particular situation. We have no evidence to suggest that these writers were aware that their work would one day be treated as scripture and read broadly. Rather, the writers of the New Testament wrote at particular times, in particular places, from particular communities, to particular audiences, and for particular circumstances.

What are the reasons for the diversity in the New Testament? Many factors are relevant. First and foremost is the fact that the life, death, and resurrection of Jesus created an explosion of fresh expressions of religious insight and social configuration. The formative events of Christianity occurred in such a way as to open up creativity rather than to close it down. These events freed people from traditional ways of thinking and produced a multiplicity of fresh experiments in communal order, ritual practices, and ethical living. The New Testament collection reflects this variety as it proliferated and spread a generation and more after the time of Jesus.

Furthermore, the writings themselves originated from Christian communities that sprang up in very different social locations. "Social location" refers to the place of a given community in society, determined by many factors: race, ethnicity, nationality, social class, economic level, political position, religious background, urban or rural origin, gender, and education. These factors shaped the distinctive perspective and purpose of each New Testament writing. We can infer features of the distinct social location of each New Testament work. Identifying social location helps us to go beyond the identification of a New Testament writing simply in terms of geographical location, time of writing, and historical circumstances. Thus, even though we may not know the person or community responsible for a given book in the New Testament, we can often infer from the writing itself a profile of the social location from which it originated.

As we have indicated, the Roman Empire encompassed an incredible diversity of nationalities, ethnic groups, languages, religions, cultures, subcultures, and races. The New Testament writings reflect the same diversity in social location. For example, among various options, we might postulate that the author of Mark wrote from a peasant perspective in rural Palestine, the author of Matthew from an educated, Jewish scribal community in urban Antioch of Syria, the author of Luke from a commitment to the poor among Gentile elites in Asia Minor, and the author of John from a marginalized Jewish group in Ephesus. Paul wrote to diverse social locations across the Mediterranean world. Thus, the writings of the New Testament were penned by people in quite different social locations.

Other factors have contributed to the diversity in the New Testament. One major factor is the diversity of authors, especially in light of the fact that scholars are uncertain whether some writings in the New Testament were written by the people to whom they are attributed. Most scholars consider it unlikely that any of the New Testament writers were themselves eyewitnesses of Jesus and that most of the writers probably did not know each other. The authors wrote different types of literature—gospel, letter, history, biography, apocalypse—and employed different styles. The authors wrote at different times, from around 50 C.E. to as late as 135 C.E., and at different places around the Mediterranean world—Galilee, Syria, Asia Minor, Greece, Macedonia, Rome, and perhaps Egypt. The writers exercised freedom in interpreting and proclaiming Jesus, because they wrote creatively to bring out the meaning of the Jesus events for their time and place. And they drew upon an even wider diversity of traditions in shaping their writings.

The authors shaped their messages to their audiences, taking into account their ethnic identity, religious background, cultural experiences, economic situation, geographical location, local interests, rural or urban ethos, and so on. The authors addressed differing historical circumstances, such as the Roman-Jewish War, the threat of persecution, a conflict with the synagogue, or the demands of the emperor cult. In addition, the authors dealt with matters internal to the life of the particular communities they addressed, such as immorality, division, domination, heresy, and laxity. Furthermore, each writing reflected the distinct Christian worldview, communal structures, and worship practices that had developed in a given location. And the audience in a given location may have had other viewpoints and traditions with which the author of a biblical writing may have disagreed.

All these and other factors produced the tremendous variety of expression in early Christianity. The result was a dizzying array of theologies about God, depictions of Jesus, views of the work of Christ, experiences of the Spirit, ethical styles, worship patterns, community structures, and understandings of salvation. The New Testament collection reflects only a sampling of this diversity, a sampling that survived through writing.

In light of this variety in the New Testament, it is not surprising that different Christian communities at different periods of history have gravitated to one writing or another as the means to find support or nurture or courage or freedom or challenge in their particular circumstances. Groups of Christians at various times seeking to respond to the challenges of their era or being persecuted for their views or disillusioned with the church or faced with poverty or confronting oppression have turned to those particular biblical stories and writings and themes that have been most helpful to them. Whether it be sixteenth-century Germans disillusioned with Catholicism or English settlers in America creating a new society or Guatemalans facing unbearable persecution from the state, Christians have turned to those parts of the New Testament that gave to them the greatest inspiration and support and challenge. In addition, Christians who are not in difficult circumstances have read the New Testament in such a way as to shape and reinforce their communal values as well as to affirm the lifestyles in which they have found themselves.

Thus, when we read the New Testament we can be aware not only of the social location of each New Testament writing but also of the social location of differing individuals and groups who read the New Testament, ourselves included. People from different situations and historical circumstances gravitate to different parts of the New Testament or read the same passages for different reasons and with different results. The diversity in the New Testament itself has made it possible for so many different people throughout history and throughout the world to find life and hope in the Christian faith. In attending to the social location of readers, we become aware of our own social location in our reading of the Bible. Such self-awareness will enable us to see the possibilities as well as the limitations and distortions that come from our own position of reading.

Eclipsing the Diversity

It quickly becomes apparent how we eclipse this diversity in the New Testament by gravitating toward certain parts of the New Testament and by focusing only on those parts of the New Testament that sustain us in our own circumstances or way of life. Because we become so accustomed to thinking of Christianity "our way," we may think our way is the only legitimate way to be Christian. Often the original reasons why a group embraced a certain form of Christianity have been forgotten, and we are no longer aware that we even have a limiting experience of the biblical faith. However, our choices are usually not coincidental but tend to affirm our own way of life and often marginalize others. Because a certain way of interpreting the Bible seems so right for us, we tend to think it is the best way or the only way for everyone. Thus, we may absolutize and universalize our experience of Christianity. In turn, we then read the whole New Testament in such a way as to reinforce our limited experiences and beliefs, perhaps even unaware that the New Testament itself embraces diversity.

In order to appreciate anew the diverse manifestations of early Christianity, it might be helpful first to see how we have eclipsed that diversity. For the most part, Christians have tended to level the diversity in the New Testament in three major ways: (1) we have harmonized the diversity by seeing the New Testament as one book in which all the writings agree with each other; (2) we have reduced the New Testament message to the lowest common denominators; and (3) we have leveled out the diversity by taking one part of the New Testament and then reading the whole New Testament through that lens, as if all the writings were saying what that one author says. Let us look more closely at each of these three ways in which we tend to level the diversity in the New Testament.

Harmonizing the Diversity

First, we tend to harmonize the New Testament writings by seeing the New Testament as one unified book rather than as a collection of writings. For example, Christians sometimes harmonize all the prophecies in the New Testament and come up with a grand scheme of our own construction, which is then applied directly as an apocalyptic scheme for our time. Unfortunately, this procedure reconfigures the view of the future as it is depicted in each individual writing and overlooks the fact that each author was applying prophecies to particular circumstances in that time. Or, when Christians talk about Jesus, we may quote from one Gospel and then from another and then from a third, as if one could put all the different stories about Jesus together and make one harmonized story. Of course this approach to Jesus is not new. The church has done this for centuries, beginning with a book called *The Diatessaron*, a harmonization of the four Gospels by a church father named Tatian in the second century.

Such harmonizing of the stories about Jesus is, in some sense, inevitable and desirable. The Gospels are stories about Jesus, and so we think of them together. We want to know what Jesus was really like, and so we make use of the sources we have. Historians who try to reconstruct a portrait of the historical Jesus sift through the different Gospels to weigh the authenticity and accuracy of the different traditions about Jesus. However, in doing this, we do not want to forget the distinctiveness of each of the Gospel writers. The Gospel writers each wrote what they considered to be an adequate portrait of Jesus, in the context of their own understanding of the human condition and their own understanding of what it means to be a disciple. In our efforts to comprehend the historical Jesus, we do not want to harmonize away the distinctiveness of the four Gospels .

An overall harmonizing of all the stories about Jesus does not work well, precisely because each Gospel writer has offered a somewhat different portrayal of Jesus. For example, in Mark's Gospel, Jesus keeps his identity a secret. His disciples do not know until halfway through the story that he is the Messiah, and no human calls him Son of God until the centurion does so at the foot of the cross. In John's Gospel, on the other hand, Jesus proclaims his identity as Son of God openly before all from the start, and early in the story his disciples know him as the lamb of God. We cannot simply put these two portraits of Jesus or the disciples together into one story. When we do, we distort both Mark and John, and we come up with a strange story unlike either one of them. The Gospel writers shaped their stories about Jesus in order to bring out the meaning of the events as they understood them. Mark is showing that Christian life is ambiguous and that people have a hard time recognizing Jesus as Son of God and accepting a persecuted Messiah, while John is showing that no matter how open Jesus is, some people will instantly recognize him and others will still not recognize that he is from God. Therefore, we need to take each story on its own terms in order to understand what each author is showing us about Jesus and the Christian life.

It can sometimes be quite misleading to harmonize different

writings into one theology. A well-known television evangelist was once asked how he justified having gold fixtures in his bathroom. His answer: "Doesn't the Bible say that the streets of Jerusalem are paved in gold? And doesn't Jesus tell us to pray, `Thy kingdom come, thy will be done on earth as it is in heaven'?" This evangelist has taken one saying from the book of Revelation, a book which offers to people who are facing persecution the hope that they will inhabit a glorious city at the second coming of Jesus, and he has misinterpreted another saying from the Gospel of Matthew, a Gospel that emphasizes the will of God for people to love the enemy and feed the hungry and clothe the naked. By putting together these two sayings out of context from two very different writings, he came up with something that is totally different from any writing in the New Testament. Indeed, this interpretation, intended to justify an opulent lifestyle, is contrary to every part of the New Testament. It is the gospel according to this evangelist, and it is not faithful to the Bible. If we combine certain views from scripture, it can be like the devil quoting scripture—the quotations or ideas come from scripture, but the combination and application of them create something unbiblical and possibly even destructive.

The example of the television evangelist is rather obvious. But to a greater or lesser degree, we all select some passages, ignore other passages, combine passages from different parts of the New Testament, and come up with a picture of Jesus of our own making. In itself, this is not wrong. However, we need to be clear that the picture we come up with is not what any one of the Gospels by itself is saying. Unfortunately, we usually end up with our own portrait of Jesus that reflects and reinforces our own social location and our own religious views. In such cases, we are not faced with visions that challenge or address us in new ways. We miss the renewal that can come by being addressed by different Gospel portrayals of Jesus. We are called to be faithful to the diversity in the New Testament.

Reducing to the Lowest Common Denominators

We also tend to eclipse the diversity in the New Testament by reducing the biblical message to a lowest common denominator, such as "Jesus is Lord" or "Jesus saves" or "Jesus is the liberator" or "God is Love." It can be helpful to seek a unifying theme across many writings in the New Testament. Such messages can be very helpful to people. People and groups live and get their identity from such powerful statements.

Such capsule statements can also be very misleading. Even if one came up with such a "New Testament in a nutshell," each writing in the New Testament would mean something different by each of those phrases mentioned above. For example, regarding the affirmation that "God is love," John understands love as a mystical relationship with God, Paul understands love as an expression of justifying grace, while other writings prefer to think of God less as love and more in terms of "holiness" (1 Peter) or "justice" (Revelation). Similarly, each writing understands Jesus' lordship and the salvation offered by Jesus in different ways. So if a community thinks of Jesus as liberator, they may miss the variety of ways in which liberation is understood throughout the New Testament. Thus, the gospel in a nutshell violates the diversity of the New Testament and inevitably becomes an oversimplification of it.

An example of reduction to a common denominator is reflected in the popular efforts to reduce the New Testament writings to a few laws or spiritual principles. Here is one such example as it appeared in the brochure of a local church:

> a. All have sinned against God's Law.
> b. The penalty for sin is death and hell.
> c. Jesus died to pay for our sins.
> d. Jesus invites us to be saved today.

Such simplified principles of salvation have undoubtedly been helpful to many people seeking relief from lives of sin and guilt. They are usually presented as if they tell the basic core of what the Bible really tells us about salvation, a sort of a summary of what all the biblical writings would agree to. However, as the following comments on these principles indicate, the matter is much more complex than this.

a. The first principle, "All have sinned against God's law," means in this tract that we as individuals have transgressed God's laws, the Ten Commandments. However, the New Testament writings depict sin in very diverse ways, including states of sin and conditions of sin, such as hypocrisy (Matthew) or fearful self-concern (Mark) or social injustice (Luke). Noting the many views of sin is crucial, because the differing ideas of sin correlate with differing views of salvation.

b. The second principle assumes that the whole New Testament expresses a belief in hell. However, the New Testament writers do not agree on an understanding of life after death. While Matthew believes that Jesus saves us from eternal punishment, Paul and John consider the future to involve the alternatives of life and death (an end to existence) rather than heaven and hell (eternal punishment). Other New Testament writings speak of Hades as the abode of the dead rather than hell, or even of Gehenna, a metaphorical reference to the waste dump of Jerusalem.

c. The third principle implies that the single purpose of Jesus was to die for people's sins to be forgiven. Yet only some writings in the New Testament depict Jesus' death as a price for people's sins to be forgiven. Luke and Mark, for example, do not show Jesus' death to be an atoning sacrifice before God; in their view, forgiveness is integral to the Christian proclamation apart from any connection to Jesus' death. And many writings in the New Testament do not depict Jesus "paying a price" for sins with his death. For example, in Luke's view, Jesus' death is depicted as the consequence of a life of obedience, and, by his death, Jesus showed followers how they too should face persecution and death. In John's view, Jesus' death and resurrection restore an alienated creation back to a relationship with God.

d. Regarding the fourth principle, the New Testament writers have different visions of the Christian life for which people have been saved: for John, it is rebirth into eternal life in the present; for Luke, it is a society of justice and mercy under the power of the Holy Spirit; and for Paul, it is communal reconciliation in a life of grace.

Thus, the effort to find a common message across many writings inevitably eclipses diversity and creates an alternative "simplified gospel," which might be helpful to people but might not accurately reflect the view of any one biblical writing by itself.

Looking at the Whole New Testament through One Lens

A third way in which we level the diversity in the New Testament is to take one part of the New Testament (usually the part important to us) and then either ignore the other writings or read all the New Testament writings through that one lens, as if all the writings agreed with what that one writing says.

Sometimes that one lens will filter out the parts of the New Testament that are not consistent with a limited vision. In American history, the "white" Christ of the southern slaveholders focused on the death of Christ as the means to individual salvation and on those biblical traditions that called for slaves to obey their masters. This lens totally eclipsed another lens, namely, the Jesus who was dedicated to healing the sick, preaching good news to the poor, and setting the prisoners free—the Jesus whom the black slaves embraced. These diverse lenses did not represent a mere innocent difference of opinion, for those who had power were able to enforce their choice and interpretation on those who were powerless. Likewise, through the centuries male scholars and preachers have read the New Testament with little awareness of the presence and contribution of women to the early church or with little understanding of how the New Testament addressed women. They, too, had the power to make their interpretation prevail. Obviously, such selective readings of the New Testament can involve tragic distortions and limitations on the work of Christ and can lead to devastating consequences for people who do not share the dominant interpretation.

At other times, the lens leads us to read the rest of the New Testament as if it agreed with our theological point of view. My own denominational context is Lutheran, and so I will use my own Lutheran tradition, initially forged out in sixteenth-century Germany, as an illustration of how we tend to view the whole New Testament through only one lens. Lutherans have as a core belief "justification by grace through faith." Lutherans (along with many other Christian groups) believe that people should not seek to justify themselves before God by doing works of the law. Rather, God has justified people through Jesus on the cross by an act of grace that destroys the power of sin to control and the power of law to convict. To live out of such grace is to trust by faith in the salvation that comes from God alone. In response to such grace, people are called to express grace and love to others out of a life of gratitude for what God has done.

Lutherans understand that this vision of salvation has its roots in Paul, primarily in Galatians and Romans. It is a legal model, and it is an understanding of life that is quite distinctive. The human condition is not primarily depicted as hypocrisy or idolatry but as the inability to establish our own righteousness before God. The goal of life is not primarily social justice or obedience to the law but reconciliation. The means to reconciliation is not forgiveness of sins or liberation from oppression but an event of justification by which God sets people right. As a depiction of the Christian life, this legal model is not found elsewhere in the New Testament. Nevertheless, Lutherans will sometimes read the whole New Testament through this one lens, as if this view were embraced by all the writers.

For example, if Lutherans regard Paul as the paradigmatic model, when we come across the term "faith" in Mark, we might think Mark means the same thing as Paul. When we came across *righteousness* in Matthew, we might infer Paul's meaning of that word. We will be mistaken, because Matthew considers righteousness to be the righteousness that God expects of people rather than the righteousness that God provides for people. Or we might treat *justification* in Luke in a Pauline fashion. But in Luke, humans are called to justify God's ways rather than to trust in God justifying humans. We will perhaps read *freedom* in John as though John were saying the same thing as Paul. But in John, freedom represents an overcoming of separation from God, not freedom from the bondage of the Law. We Lutherans often come to a passage in the New Testament with the Lutheran-Pauline categories of law and gospel, grace and faith. Then, when we preach, we approach a passage in the Gospels by determining first where the law is to be found in that passage and then where the gospel is to be found that addresses the people under law. The problem, however, is that the categories of law and gospel may actually be alien to the passage we are studying. The result is that we will hear Pauline sermons on Matthew, Pauline sermons on Luke, Pauline sermons on John, and so on!

Examples can be multiplied from other Christian communities. Some evangelical communities read the whole New Testament as if all authors agreed with the hierarchy of household roles, whereby wives are to be subject to their husbands, found in Colossians (3:18–4:1), Ephesians (5:21–6:9), and 1 Peter (2:18–3:7), even though these are the only writings that contain them and even though other writings emphasize a mutuality of roles (e.g., Mark 10:28–45; 1 Corinthians 7:1–39). Others will read the Bible as if the admonition to be subject to the government (Romans 13:1–7) represented the views of all authors. On the contrary, there are admonitions to obey God rather than human authorities (for example, Acts 4:19), as witnessed by the fact that the apostles spent a lot of time in prison. Still others read the whole New Testament as if all writers agreed with the future apocalyptic scheme of the book of Revelation, even though many New Testament writings put forward the notion that the endtime has already begun in the present.

Now, in one sense, it need not be inappropriate to read the whole New Testament in light of the Pauline prism or any other particular prism. Pauline concepts can be expanded more broadly to encompass other biblical views. For example, we may speak of God's prior action (grace) and our human response (faith). Evaluating all the writings from this particular point of view can be illuminating and clarifying of similarities and differences, but *only* if we first know what the other writings say on their own terms. What is problematic is the tendency to level all the writings under one point of view and flatten out the rich diversity. In the sixteenth century, Martin Luther generally read the New Testament on Pauline terms. When he came to the letter of James, Luther found the emphasis on justification by works to be so incompatible with justification by grace, that he called James "the epistle of straw" and suggested that it should not be in the New Testament. And the letter of James is not the only New Testament writing that may be problematic for Lutherans. Other writings may be more or less compatible with Paul, but they are all different in theology and conception from Paul. We could just as easily read the whole New Testament through the prism of a Matthean or of a Lukan model of salvation, as other denominations do, and be just as firmly based on the Bible.

This elevation of one writing or theology or theme in the New Testament is called "a canon within the canon." The word *canon* refers to the particular books that are considered to be scripture and that are authoritative for the life and faith of Christians. The writings in the New Testament comprise the New Testament

canon for Christian groups. Yet, at the same time, each denominational and cultural expression of Christianity will emphasize
some writings within the New Testament as more authoritative
for their life and faith than other writings—hence a "canon within
the canon." Clearly, each group can elevate certain traditions and
also read other traditions on their own terms. The problem comes
when we eclipse the diversity or flatten the rest of the New Testament through the myopic vision of a single lens.

Accepting the Diversity

Once we see that the biblical writings are so diverse that no one
group can live them all, we come to accept the diversity among us
Christians today as inevitable, indeed as salutary. If we do not harmonize or simplify or level out the biblical writings, we come to
understand that it takes many different kinds of Christian groups
to bear the full biblical witness in the modern world. In fact, the
biblical materials are so diverse that choice is unavoidable. A community cannot emphasize for their life together *everything* that the
New Testament says. Each group will emphasize some theologies
or ethical principles or church organization or rites within the New
Testament and ignore or disagree with others. Thus, Christian
communities of differing social locations will have their own
canon or canons within the New Testament—in practice if not in
explicit belief. To state it in a positive way, we have a situation in
which each group selects some biblical traditions for itself and
then is able to honor, indeed, to depend on other Christian groups
for living out of other biblical traditions in their life together.

The inevitability of choice becomes obvious when one sees how
various denominations or various cultural, ethnic, and gender
groups within denominations have in fact appropriated the Bible.
The Roman Catholic church has drawn heavily upon the church
organization represented in Matthew and the catholic epistles.
Some evangelical groups lift up the experience of being reborn
described in the Gospel of John. The Pentecostal traditions hold up
the emphasis in Acts and 1 Corinthians on the baptism in the Holy
Spirit and the diverse gifts of the Spirit, especially speaking in
tongues. Many African Americans appeal to the letter of James as a
manifesto to end discrimination and economic oppression. Hispanic communities emphasizing liberation may focus on the social

transformations in the Gospel of Mark or the Gospel of Luke. The Christian Science tradition looks at the New Testament through the prism of Jesus' healings. The Anabaptist traditions lean upon the ethics of the Sermon on the Mount. These are only some of the most obvious examples of the realities of choice and interpretation among denominations and groups within denominations.

The point is that each denomination and each ethnic group within particular denominations can celebrate their distinctive traditions and still be renewed by the traditions of others and by the diversity in the New Testament. Thus, there is more than one way to be faithful to the biblical materials. Here we are free to make choices without being exclusive and without thinking we have a corner on the truth. To say that we are right is not to say that others are wrong. We are called to make choices in a responsible way, in our relation with God and together with folks around us, about how we will be faithful to the biblical witnesses. At the same time, the experience of biblical traditions other than our own can make us aware of our limitations or misinterpretations or imbalances and can broaden and deepen our understanding of the biblical tradition. However, the idea is not to choose one or the other tradition as correct or incorrect but to open ourselves to interpretations that go beyond our own. In the process we may also come to appreciate contemporary groups that hold other texts and practices to be authoritative.

Here, then, is an appeal for each expression of Christianity to be faithful to its own core tradition for the sake of the whole catholic church—for Methodists to be faithful to the New Testament traditions that have shaped them, for Native American Christians to be faithful to the diverse New Testament traditions that have shaped them, for African American Christians to be faithful to the traditions that have shaped them, for Pentecostals to be faithful to their New Testament traditions, Presbyterians to their biblical traditions, Baptists to be faithful to their biblical traditions, for all people to be faithful to the traditions that have sustained and empowered their communities, and at the same time to celebrate other New Testament writings and traditions on their own terms and to learn from them—even within the same denomination. In this way, each community can be distinctive for the benefit of the whole church and still embrace diversity. Many denominations already embrace considerable diversity, yet rediscovering the diversity in the Bible can make us aware of the limitations and exclusiveness of our own tradition. At the same time, appreciating the biblical spectrum of Christianity can provide resources for the renewal of each church and of the whole church in its mission in the world today.

Embracing the Diversity

Once we accept the diversity in the New Testament and value it, we can embrace its many possibilities for renewal. Here is a collection of writings each of which cuts profoundly to the heart of the human condition in a whole variety of ways. How much more interesting the Christian venture is when there are many models for understanding and living. The guidance for community is more helpful when we realize that the earliest testimonies reveal many experiments in life together. The reflection and imagination of Christians is enriched when we see that the foundational visions manifested multiform ways to understand God and the work of Christ. The promise of the Christian mission is greater when we draw upon diverse examples of the Christian life for renewal. The hope for the church's work in the world is enhanced when there is such a wide variety of resources to guide us in facing ever new and changing circumstances. The freedom and confidence to chart our own course grows when we see how the writers of the New Testament took up the challenge to shape the Christian message to particular circumstances and audiences. Our respect for ethnic and cultural diversity expands when we realize how many different cultural expressions of Christianity are already built into the New Testament itself. Our spiritual revival is deepened when we are addressed with insights from such varied writings. The meaning of our life as a church is broadened when we know that there are contemporary expressions among us of the diversity that is present in the New Testament itself.

Reading for Diversity

One major key to our renewal is that we read and interpret each biblical writing on its own terms rather than looking at them all through our own perspective. It is tempting to read and interpret so as to serve our own theology or our own group. However, it can be challenging and rewarding to read so as to let the texts speak for themselves and thereby address us in fresh ways. We may even need to learn the practice of listening carefully in order for the biblical writings to bear their greatest fruit with us. A story articulates well the limitations of attending only to our own perspective:

> One foggy night at sea the captain of a ship saw what looked like the lights of another ship heading toward him. He had his signalman contacted the other ship by light. The message was: "Change your course ten degrees to the south."
>
> The reply came back: "Change your course ten degrees to the north."
>
> Then the captain answered: "I am a captain, so you change your course ten degrees to the south."
>
> Reply: "I am a seaman first class—change your course ten degrees to the north."
>
> This last exchange really infuriated the captain, so he signaled back: "I am a battleship—change your course ten degrees to the south."
>
> Reply: "And I am a lighthouse. Change your course ten degrees to the north!"

As readers of scripture, we often find ourselves like the captain of that ship, seeing only from our own perspective, seeing the lighthouse as though it were a ship so that we can move it around to where we want it to be or make it say what we want it to say. But the text will not move, and if we are not careful we will run aground. Our problem is that we do not know the larger lay of the land. If we knew the larger picture—what the landscape was like—we would know that a lighthouse stood before us. And the passage of scripture would then become what it was truly meant to be—a beacon that sheds new light on our human situation. However, we do not need our own perspective as much as we need the perspective from the lighthouse, the framework provided by the writing, to properly experience the passage as a lighthouse. Each writing as a whole provides the appropriate framework for interpreting the passages from within that writing. When we use the writing as a whole to provide the lay of the land, we will see a passage of Mark in the context of the Markan landscape and a passage from Luke in the context of the Lukan landscape.

In light of the need to know landscapes other than our own, how might we read the New Testament so as to see clearly the distinctiveness of each writing? Renewal for the church comes from the Bible when we experience the "otherness" of each writing. Renewal seldom comes by experiencing the passage as an extension of ourselves. When we see the passage as an extension of ourselves, we see in it only what we already think or expect to see in it. However, we can learn how to read for diversity. Basically, in order to do that, we need to stay with a biblical writing until it is different from what we already think it will be. When we unravel its strangeness, when we stay open to the "otherness" of each biblical writing, then it addresses us in fresh ways. Here are five guidelines on reading for diversity.

1. Read each writing as a whole.

We are so used to reading or hearing bits and pieces of scripture. Seldom do we read a whole writing at one sitting. It is somewhat like hearing many quotations from Shakespeare but never having seen a whole play. However, the basic unit of meaning for interpreting a quotation of scripture is the individual writing. Read each gospel as you would read a play or a novel or a short story. Read each writing at one sitting and get immersed in it. Follow the characters, trace the conflicts, see how the story is brought to a resolution. Think of yourself as entering the world of the writing as you might get lost in a novel or, even better, as you might enter the world of a story in a film. You go into the theater, the lights are lowered, and you are drawn into the world of the story. You experience the story that the characters experience, you see the world as the characters see it, and you may be changed by the experience. When we do this with the Bible, we see that each writing has its own unique world, and we appreciate each of these worlds in its integrity. Each writing as a whole has its own distinctive portrayal of Jesus and the Christian life. Then when we read individual passages, we can understand their meaning in the context of the larger framework, the larger landscape, of that writing as a whole. As you read this book, you may want to set it as a goal to read each biblical writing under consideration in its entirety at one sitting.

2. Expect to be surprised.

The writings of the New Testament were penned two thousand

years ago in very different cultural settings and under vastly different historical circumstances from our own. Reading the New Testament is a cross-cultural experience into a different world of honor and shame, purity and pollution, angels and demons, communal identity and an experience of limited economic goods. Undoubtedly, the social location of a New Testament writing was very different from our own. The diversity was so fundamental that each writer displays a different vision for human life under God. If we expect we already know what each writing of the Bible has to say, chances are we will find what we expect to find and we will simply reinforce what we already believe. But if we are prepared to look closely, to listen carefully, to expect the unexpected, and to encounter diversity, we will not be disappointed: we will be surprised and puzzled and challenged and even disturbed. Indeed, if we are not surprised, we should probably go back and read it again!

3. Look for the underlying ideas and standards in each work.

What is at the heart of each work? What makes it unique? What is possible in its world? What is it like to see the world as this writer sees it? It is helpful to look for the standards of judgment, the values and beliefs by which the author leads us as readers to evaluate the people as being either good or bad, right or wrong. In general the biblical writers thought in dualistic terms. There was a right way and a wrong way, and the right way mirrored the wrong way by contrast, so that the right way and the wrong way illuminated each other as mirror opposites. The wrong way represents the writer's view of our human condition. The right way represents that author's vision of what God calls people to become. For example, in Matthew, the human condition is hypocrisy that destroys community, whereas God's goal for humans is life together with integrity. In John, the human condition is the failure to know God, and the vision for life is to know God in an intimate and spiritual way. In Luke, the human condition is society without mercy, and the vision for life is society with mercy. In addition, for each writing there will then be a different view of salvation that coheres with the particular analysis of the human condition and with the particular vision for life. So we can ask of each writing: In this writing, how does God bring transformation so that people are delivered from the human condition for the life God wants people to live? The general framework that emerges becomes the landscape for interpreting individual passages from that writing. Based on this analysis, we can begin to "Think Matthean" or to "Think as a Lukan Christian."

4. Read with others.

It is amazing how much we can learn from reading the Bible with others. Even when we read the Bible in a group of people much like ourselves, people seem to notice different things about a biblical passage and to find diverse ways to relate it to their own lives. Beyond this, if we read the Bible only with people from our own denominational, cultural, economic, political, ethnic, or gender group, we may be unaware of how limited we are in what we see and in how we relate to the text. Different people will read the very same text in different ways because they are coming from different social locations.

The importance of reading with others came home most clearly to me at an international conference on "Cultural Interpretation." The program featured thirty-five speakers from different countries around the world sharing their perspectives on reading the Bible—including people from China, Korea, India, Ethiopia, South Africa, Israel, Palestine, the United States, Brazil, Argentina, along with a Native American, a Mayan Indian, and an Australian aborigine. Especially fascinating were people whose cultures were more like the ancient biblical culture than Western cultures are. These interpreters seemed to have an inside track for understanding honor and shame, purity and defilement, illness and demons, and communal life. People who came from situations of oppression saw clearly how much of the Bible was written from the perspective of the poor and the oppressed. This enabled them to relate in a vital way to the Bible, because stories and sayings lit up their situation, and in turn their own situation illuminated the biblical stories. We can look forward to reading with others different from ourselves because we can expect to have our understanding of the Bible broadened and deepened.

By reading with others, we become aware of the possibilities and limitations of the social location from which we read, and we are able to attend to the possibilities and limitations offered by people who come from different social locations. We learn not only *that* social location shapes our interpretations but also *how* it shapes our interpretations. In addition, we can see more clearly how those with power and influence, those on the inside, tend to determine which interpretations and methods of reading will prevail in the given culture. By overcoming one group's claim to privilege, by decentering prevailing interpretations, and by learning to read from the margins, communities can challenge and be challenged by reading with one another.

5. Be honest.

If we want to see the Bible as presenting something different from what we already believe and do as Christians, we will want to be in frank dialogue with the biblical writings, expressing our honest responses to and struggles with the different writings. Otherwise, when we come across something we do not like or disagree with, we will tend to make it say what agrees with us or to soften its offense so that it sounds "reasonable" or to pretend it is not there. It would be better for us to be honest about the fact that we resist a certain part of the New Testament or that we disagree with it or that we think it is not appropriate for our time or that it may lead to harm. Such honesty will lead us to probe more deeply and perhaps to see the writing in a new light. We may not always embrace the diversity we meet, but we can still deal with it seriously and learn from our struggle with it. Only as we honestly see a writing in the New Testament as new and challenging are we able to be addressed with words that might transform us.

Here, then, are some suggestions about how to work beyond our own limitations so as to read the Bible in order to hear the voices of the biblical writers on their own terms, to read for diversity. The same kinds of guidelines for listening are helpful also in the whole process of listening to the voices of each other as we are challenged by reading together, as we agree and differ in our interpretations of what we read.

Reading for Renewal

Ultimately, reading for renewal means to allow ourselves to be changed, to read with the expectation of being transformed, to read in the hope of being a new people. The biblical writings themselves were penned in order to be vehicles for the power of God, in order to grasp readers, to reorient them, to evoke responses, to create wholeness, to engender action on behalf of others. In a sense, the writings are not fully interpreted until their visions take shape in our lives and in our communities. Ultimately, then, the biblical writings lead not just to interpretation but to action, to changed relationships, and to new communities. There is a "spirituality of the Word" involved in this kind of openness— a willingness to question one's own views, to entertain other ways of being Christian, with an eagerness for the insights of others, a readiness to be transformed ever anew, and a commitment to change our behavior.

Many approaches could be taken to unpacking the diversity in the New Testament in an even more encompassing way than our approach here. The limited approach of this book will be to look at the diversity among five different writings in the New Testament. We will be looking at Paul's letter to the Galatians, the Gospel of Mark, the Gospel of Matthew, the Gospel of Luke, and the Gospel of John (the probable order in which they were written). Although we will refer to the authors of these works, our focus is on the writings themselves and the way the authors have invested themselves in their writings.

The core of each chapter seeks to show the coherence in each writing between the human condition, the vision for life, and the means of salvation. My focus is on the vision for *this* life in each of the writings, although, to be sure, New Testament writers promise a future resurrected life after death and this will be part of our analysis. Near the end of each chapter, there are examples of historical "trajectories" of each writing, including some ways in which various faith communities from different social locations have found this particular biblical tradition to be meaningful and supportive of their life together. In addition, the end of each chapter depicts an imaginary example of a contemporary Christian community that reflects that particular biblical writing. Such reflections are meant to stimulate you to draw upon your own knowledge of the Christian life and to be imaginative in thinking about how *you* might relate this writing to the contemporary world. Each chapter concludes with a bibliography that reflects a diversity of interpretation from different social locations. At the end of the book are questions for each chapter designed to open up discussion about the way in which each writing might shape the life of our communities today.

I am aware of the relative and limited nature of my own interpretations, coming as they are from my particular social location. Other interpreters of scripture from similar or different social locations will depict the distinctiveness of each of these writings in ways different from the views presented here. Such multiform interpretations are crucial for understanding the Bible, and they serve to enhance the rich diversity already there in the New Testament. Differing interpretations of the same passages and books are just as crucial for diversity as the choices of different passages that shape our life together.

In choosing to highlight the dualistic standards of each writing, I have chosen to focus on one main thrust of each work. That is, I have chosen to emphasize some things and not deal with other things. The New Testament writings are rich and complex, and the following brief studies do not begin to deal fully with the dynamics within each one of them. Also, for the purposes of this book, I have chosen to highlight what is distinctive about each Gospel. At the same time, I recognize that the four Gospels hold much in common. This brief study, then, is an effort to place in sharp relief a basic theological framework for each of five New Testament writings. The method will be to focus not on attempting to discern the actual historical Jesus but on the *portrayals* of Jesus in these different writings. My hope is that this experience will generate a greater awareness of diversity in the Bible and perhaps initiate a process of reading that will enable the biblical writings to work their renewal upon us.

An Explanatory Note on the Use of the Term "Judeans"

In studying the New Testament, there is a danger of being drawn into a tragic anti-Judaism. In their dualistic framework of thinking, New Testament writers usually associated one Jewish group or another with the negative side of the dualism. In dealing with this dualism, it is important for us to keep in mind that Jesus himself was a Jew, the earliest Christians were Jews, and the conflicts of Christians with other Jewish groups were directed not against all Jews (then or now) or against Judaism as such. Later, Gentile Christians read the earlier intrafaith conflicts between two Jewish groups anachronistically as if they were conflicts between two different religions, Jews and Christians. The depictions of Jews in the Gospels come to us filtered through Christian lenses and do not show the opponents speaking for themselves. In addition, the portrayals of Jewish groups in the Gospels tend toward being stereotypical characterizations meant to show readers two ways of life, and they do not depict the Jewish groups of that time as we know them from other sources. Finally, the New Testament writings, penned by a small, powerless, and nonviolent sect, became the scriptures of a large, dominant worldwide religion, which has often used those writings to justify almost twenty centuries of Christian anti-Judaism, expressed in persistent prejudice, repeated persecution, and, in our time, massive, systematic destruction. How ironic that a nonviolent sect should become a violent religion—against the very religion from which it emerged and with whom we have so much in common. Clearly, our situation as Christians calls for soul-searching, repentance, and a determined repudiation of anti-Judaism.

As readers, we are called to read the New Testament so that we do not universalize the particular controversies of the first century and make them into a clash between religions in our very different context. As a reminder of this, we will refer in the remainder of this book to biblical Jews by their proper first-century designation, "Judeans"—that is, people who lived in the region of Judea in southern Palestine (in contrast to Galilee) or people who lived in the overall province of Judea (in contrast to Judeans who lived outside Palestine) or people who lived elsewhere but originated from Judea or people who embraced the religion of Judea. The context of each occurrence of our use of the word will make clear which meaning of "Judeans" prevails in any given use. In a study like this one, devoted to openness and an embracing of differences, it would be very unfortunate if we as readers were not able to see Judaism as a vital and independent witness to the work of God from whom we as Christians have much to learn.

Further Reading

Aichele, George, et al. *The Postmodern Bible: The Bible and the Culture Collective*. New Haven: Yale University Press, 1995.

Albanese, Catherine. *America: Religions and Religion*. Belmont, Calif.: Wadsworth, 1992.

Beck, Norman. *Mature Christianity in the 21st Century: The Recognition and Repudiation of the Anti-Jewish Polemic of the New Testament*. New York: Crossroad, 1994.

Blount, Bryan. *Cultural Interpretation: Reorienting New Testament Criticism*. Minneapolis: Fortress Press 1995.

Countryman, William. *Biblical Authority or Tyranny? Scripture and the Christian Pilgrimage*. Philadelphia: Fortress Press, 1981.

Crockett, Joseph. *Teaching Scripture from an African American Perspective*. Nashville: Discipleship Resources, 1990.

Crossan, John Dominic. *Who Killed Jesus? Exposing the Roots of Anti-Judaism in the Gospel Story of the Death of Jesus*. San Francisco: Harper, 1995.

Douglas, Kelly. *The Black Christ*. Maryknoll: Orbis, 1995.

Dunn, James. *Unity and Diversity in the New Testament: An Inquiry into the Character of Earliest Christianity.* 2d edition. Philadelphia: Trinity Press International, 1990.

Evans, Craig and Donald Hagner, editors. *Anti-Semitism and Early Christian Faith: Issues of Polemic and Faith.* Minneapolis: Fortress Press, 1993.

Fiorenza, Elisabeth Schüssler, editor. *Searching the Scriptures: A Feminist Introduction.* New York: Crossroad, 1993.

The Gospel in Solentiname. 4 volumes. Maryknoll: Orbis, 1976–1982.

Gottwald, Norman and Richard Horsley, editors. *The Bible and Liberation: Political and Social Hermeneutics,* revised edition. Maryknoll: Orbis, 1993.

Hagen, Kenneth, et al., editors. *The Bible in the Churches: How Different Christians Read Scripture.* Mahwah, N.J.: Paulist Press, 1985.

Hanson, Paul. *The Diversity of Scripture: A Theological Interpretation.* Philadelphia: Fortress Press, 1982.

Jobling, David, et al., editors. *The Bible and the Politics of Exegesis.* Cleveland: Pilgrim Press, 1991.

Malina, Bruce. *The New Testament World: Insights from Cultural Anthropology.* 2d edition. Louisville: Westminster/John Knox, 1993.

Malina, Bruce and Richard Rohrbaugh. *A Social-Science Commentary on the Synoptic Gospels.* Minneapolis: Fortress Press, 1992.

Melton, Gordon. *The Encyclopedia of American Religions.* Detroit: Gale Research, 1989.

Mesters, Carlos. *Defenseless Flower: A New Reading of the Bible.* Maryknoll: Orbis, 1989.

Neyrey, Jerome. *Paul, In Other Words: A Cultural Reading of His Letters.* Louisville: Westminster/John Knox, 1990.

Patte, Daniel. *Ethics of Biblical Interpretation: A Reevaluation.* Louisville: Westminster/John Knox, 1995.

Pero, Albert and Ambrose Moyo, editors. *Theology and the Black Experience.* Minneapolis: Fortress Press, 1988.

Reumann, John. *Variety and Unity in New Testament Thought.* Oxford: Oxford University Press, 1991.

Rowley, H. H. *The Unity of the Bible.* Philadelphia: Westminster, 1953.

Russell, Keith. *In Search of the Church: New Testament Images for Tomorrow's Congregations.* New York: Alban Institute, 1994.

Segovia, Fernando and Mary Ann Tolbert, editors. *Reading from This Place: Social Location and Biblical interpretation in the United States,* volume 1. Minneapolis: Fortress Press, 1995.

————. *Reading from This Place: Social Location and Biblical Interpretation in Global Perspective,* volume 2. Minneapolis: Fortress Press, 1995.

Smiga, George. *Pain and Polemic: Anti-Judaism in the Gospels.* New York: Paulist, 1992.

Smith-Christopher, Daniel, editor. *Text and Experience: Toward a Cultural Exegesis of the Bible.* Sheffield: Sheffield Academic Press, 1995.

Tamez, Elsa. *The Bible of the Oppressed*. Maryknoll: Orbis, 1982.

West, Gerald. *Biblical Hermeneutics of Liberation: Modes of Reading the Bible in the South African Context*. Pietermaritzburg, South Africa: Cluster Publications, 1991.

White, Benton. *Taking the Bible Seriously*. Louisville: Westminster/ John Knox, 1993.

Williams, Newell, editor. *A Case Study of Mainstream Protestantism: The Disciples' Relation to American Culture*. Grand Rapids: Eerdmans, 1989.

Williams, Peter. *America's Religions: Traditions and Cultures*. New York: Macmillan, 1990.

Young, Pamela Dickey. *Christ in a Post-Christian World*. Minneapolis: Fortress Press, 1995.

2
Galatians
Justification by Grace

Background and Purpose

IN THE EARLY FIFTIES OF THE FIRST CENTURY, Paul was traveling through the territory of Galatia in central Asia Minor, a predominantly rural region under the aegis of the Roman Empire. Residents were Gentiles, probably from the lower classes. On his journey, Paul became ill with a malady that affected his eyes (4:13–15). When some Galatians welcomed him and cared for him, Paul preached to them the gospel that God had saved all people from this evil age of strife and division for a life of reconciliation together under God. God had done this through the death of the Judean Messiah Jesus, and they as Gentiles were now justified before God through their faith in this act of God's grace. Because of God's unconditional grace, these Gentiles need not follow the Law of Israel in order to be saved from this evil age, for they would become children and inheritors of Abraham by virtue of their faith. They were called in the Spirit to live an ethical life of love consistent with the gracious act of God in Christ. When Paul preached, the grace of God was confirmed among the Galatians by the gift of the Spirit, which brought miracles and other dramatic signs of God's work among them (3:1–4). Paul founded several Christian communities in the region and then moved on to establish other congregations elsewhere.

After Paul left, there came to Galatia some Judean Christian missionaries (1:6–7), who believed that in order to be saved by the Judean Messiah Jesus, people had to become *Judean* followers of Jesus; that is, males were to be circumcised and everyone was to obey the moral and ritual ordinances in the Law of Moses—the Torah, the first five books of the Old Testament. These missionaries may have asked the Galatians, Did God not give the Law to Moses? Did people stop sinning after they became Christians (2:17)? Did they not still need the Law? As a result, some Galatian Christians were circumcised and kept Judean days of observance (4:10; 5:3).

In order to persuade the Galatians of their views, these missionaries sought to discredit Paul and his apostleship. We can infer what these opponents probably said from the way Paul defends himself. First, they said that Paul was not a genuine apostle, because he had never known Jesus (1:11–12). Second, they said that Paul got his gospel secondhand from the apostles who had known Jesus (1:16–23). Finally, they accused Paul of preaching to please people by offering a gospel that did not require obedience to the Judean Law (1:10).

When Paul heard what his opponents were saying, he dictated this letter to reclaim the Galatian Christians for the gospel of grace and freedom from Law. In his letter, Paul countered the arguments of the Judean Christian missionaries. First, he claimed that he was a true apostle who had been called directly by the risen Jesus through the grace of God (1:11–12). Second, he claimed that he got his gospel firsthand from God through the risen Jesus and not from humans, not even indirectly through the apostles in Jerusalem (1:1; 11–17). Besides, he argued, it was not until years after his encounter with the risen Jesus that he even saw the other apostles, and when he did consult with them they approved his gospel (1:16–2:10). Finally, he claimed that he could hardly be preaching a gospel to please people or he would not have been persecuted so severely and would not bear the marks of Christ on his body (1:10; 5:11; 6:17). Then, in the bulk of the letter, Paul argued from the Law itself in the scriptures (the Old Testament) and from experience to defend his gospel of unconditional grace. He ended his letter with a ringing declaration of the freedom of Christians in the Holy Spirit to live a life of love apart from Law.

"Justification by grace through faith" was Paul's vision of God's righteous plan to redeem and to reconcile all the diverse peoples of the world. Justification is a legal term that refers to one who stands acquitted or vindicated before a judge's tribunal. For Paul, being justified implied that one's relationships with God and people were right and righteous. In Paul's view, *how* one is justified before God is the key to all ethical relationships. When God justified people through Christ, Paul argued, God was saving people from destructive ways of justifying themselves and saving them for a life of mutual love and reconciliation. According to Paul, justification by grace was the way God acted to bring about justice in the world.

Paul believed that God worked through Israel to establish a justification that transcended the particularity of the Law of Israel as the means to become justified before God. It is central to Paul's thought that God is impartial and will keep the promises to the nations as well as the promises to Israel (3:8). When Paul first preached in a Gentile area, he announced that Gentiles were heirs to the promises given to Abraham without having to follow the laws of the Judeans—circumcision, Sabbath, festivals, observance of the new moon, along with extensive moral and legal prescriptions. Without prerequisites, Paul argued, the Gentile nations were now heirs to the promises of justification, the Spirit, and salvation, because in Jesus' death God broke the power of sin and set people right(eous) before God. Jesus was the end of the Law as an effort to gain salvation and the beginning of living in response to the Spirit as an expression of a justification already granted through Christ.

In Paul's view, Judeans who became Christians could continue or not continue to carry out the Law as their cultural expression of Christian life, knowing full well that this did not save them (2:15–16). When Paul preached to Judeans, he acted, along with Peter and others who preached to their fellow Judeans, as one under the Law (1 Corinthians 9:20–23). However, in Paul's view, there was no legitimate reason for Gentiles to adopt the Law. It was not a cultural expression of their life. For Gentiles to adopt the Law could only mean that they thought it was required for salvation. Paul proclaimed that people were saved through faith. Just as the promises to Abraham had been free, so now justification is free, and Gentiles could and should receive it without following the Jewish Law. With this theology of freedom, Paul assured people in different Gentile cultures around the Mediterranean that they could be saved without being assimilated into the culture of the nation of Israel.

In his letters,[1] Paul deals with the theology of justification only where there is a controversy about whether Gentiles were to adopt the Law of Israel. In the letter to the Galatians, for example, Paul deals with justification because Judean-Christian missionaries tried to subvert Paul's views. In the letter to the Philippians, he deals with justification briefly in order to counter opponents there who sought to require the Law of Moses for Gentiles who became Christians. In the letter to the Romans, Paul deals with justification because he seeks to reconcile conflicts between Judean-Christians and Gentile-Christians in Rome. We are fortunate, therefore, to have Paul's letters to the Galatians and to the Romans, because there Paul develops in a comprehensive way his theology of justification as a contrast between life under Law and life in response to grace.[2] In this chapter, the focus will be on Galatians, with occasional references to Paul's other letters.[3]

The Two Ways: Justification by Works of Law or Justification by Grace

In the letter to the Galatians, there are fundamentally two ways— life under the law and life as response to grace. Life lived by law represents one way of relating to God and to other people. For Paul, following law is not the basis upon which people will stand justified before God or be righteous in relation to other people. By contrast, living in response to the unconditional grace of God is liberating. By grace one already stands justified/righteous before God, and by the ongoing gift of the Spirit one can be righteous in relation to others. Therefore, for Paul, the two ways, each of which mirrors the other by contrast, are life lived under law as a means to gain justification and life lived through faith in response to grace as a means of justification. In his comprehensive treatment of justification in Galatians, Paul has a thoroughgoing application of this theology at the level of nations and cultures, at the level of life together in a community, and at the individual level of one's relationship with God and other people.

In Galatians, Paul deals with justification by works in terms of the Judean Law. However, by suggestion and implication, Paul condemns the view that *any* human achievement or status can be the basis for justifying oneself before God. Ask yourself in what ways you seek to prove or justify your worth as a person before God and before other people: Do you do it by goodness, generosity, importance, position of power, influence, wealth, achievements, or some other criterion of self-worth? For Paul, this would be a salvation rooted in human effort or "the flesh." Paul claims that neither ascribed statuses from birth such as gender and social class nor acquired statuses such as education and wisdom are any basis for justifying oneself before God (see 1 Corinthians 1:26–31). Thus, seeking justification by good works of the Law of Israel is one illustrative example of seeking to justify oneself by human achievement. In this chapter, we will use "law" (lower-case) to refer in a generic sense to any standards by which people seek to justify themselves; and we will use "Law" (upper-case) to refer to the ordinances of Israel, which according to tradition were given to Moses on Mount Sinai. In contrast to justification by human achievement, Paul preaches a justification by grace through faith made possible by God's action in Christ.

Here is a chart of the two ways in Galatians:

Justification by Works of Law	*Justification by Grace*
Living up to the Law	Living in response to grace
Seeking self-justification	Responding to God's justification
Human achievement (works)	Faith in God's action (grace)
Flesh (person separated from God)	God's Spirit (transforms person)
Law restrains immorality	Spirit produces righteousness
Living under the curse (of the Law)	Having the blessing (of Abraham)
Slave to Law (children of Hagar)	Free (children of Abraham / Sarah)
Works of flesh	Fruits of the Spirit
Destructive (manipulate people)	Life-bringing (love for sake of other)
Results in boasting and envy	Results in love for the neighbor
Division	Unity
Death (corruption)	Life (eternal)
This present evil age	New creation

The Human Condition: Life under Law

In Paul's view, the efforts of people to carry out the works of God's Law as the means to justify themselves before God and as the way to achieve righteousness in relation to other people are doomed to failure—for at least five reasons.

First, Paul argues that one can never be justified before God by doing works of the Law, because no one can carry out all the demands of the Law. "I testify that if anyone becomes circumcised he is obliged to obey the whole law" (5:3). The result of failing to obey the whole law is that one is under a curse, a curse of punishment that failure to keep the Law entails (the opposite of blessing). "Those who are people of works of the law are under a curse. As it is written, 'Cursed is everyone who does not stay with everything which is written in the book of the law to keep it' " (3:10, quoting Deuteronomy 27:26). Paul concluded that "It is obvious that no one is justified before God by doing works of the law" (3:11). For Paul, those who choose to live by Law make it a way of life, for "Whoever does them [the laws] shall live by them" (3:11). Because people cannot carry out the whole Law, they come under the curse of the Law (4:25).[4]

Second, even the fulfillment of the Law does not bring justification, because the entire effort to gain God's acceptance by proving oneself is a misconceived project (2:15–16). Rooting salvation in human efforts is to no avail (3:1–5), as if one could put God in human debt (see Romans 4:4–5; 11:35): "If I am a good person, God will be obligated to reward me." Such a self-centered attitude is not love for God. Hence, even success in carrying out the Law fails to attain justification, for "the righteous shall live by faith" (3:11). As Paul says elsewhere, "Whatever does not proceed from faith is sin" (Romans 14:23).

Paul's own story confirms this, for Paul fundamentally succeeded in following the Law. "I advanced," he writes, " beyond many among my people who were of the same age, since I was far more zealous for the traditions of my ancestors" (1:14). Elsewhere, he describes himself as one who had been "blameless" in regard to the Law (Philippians 3:6). Nevertheless, Paul discovered through his encounter with the risen Jesus that he had been living *directly contrary to God* by persecuting the church of Christ (1:13–14, 23). After he experienced the grace of the resurrected Jesus (1:15–16), Paul looked back and described his "successful" life under the Law as contrary to God's will (2:15), indeed, as so much rubbish (Philippians 3:7–11). Now he desired to know only Christ, the power of his resurrection, and the fellowship of his sufferings, because these things brought life and true righteousness.

There is a difference between Paul's experience and that of Martin Luther, the sixteenth-century reformer of the church who based his theology on Paul's idea of justification by grace through faith. This Augustinian monk agonized over every tiny fault and could not confess enough sins before his confessor to assure himself that he was acceptable to God. Luther found a gracious God who provided justification in the face of his *failure* to justify himself by works of law. By contrast, Paul was rescued from the *success* of keeping the Law—a success that, when looked at from Paul's experience of Christ, did not produce righteousness. So whether one fails at keeping the Law as Luther did or succeeds at keeping the Law as Paul did, the whole effort to keep the law as a means to justification is contrary to the way God wills for people to relate to God.

This observation perhaps explains why Paul preached justification and not forgiveness. If a person is forgiven for certain failures, the assumption may be that the overall project to please God based on law is legitimate and that one simply needs to be forgiven where one fails. In this view, people try to make themselves right with God by carrying out the law, and where they fail, God will forgive them. However, people are still basically seeking to be justified before God by human effort—and they get by with some forgiveness from God. By contrast, Paul argues that it is a contradiction to seek to attain by human effort what God freely gives by grace.

Third, laws do not give a person the desire or capacity to carry out what they command: "If a law were written that was capable of making alive, then righteousness would indeed come through law" (3:21). In Paul's view, the Law does not bring life; the Spirit does (see Romans 8:1–11). From Moses to Christ, the Law had served only as a temporary disciplinarian (3:19–24). The Law was good, but it was neither a requirement for nor a means of salvation. The Law could restrain people from negative immorality by its threat of punishment; but the Law could not produce positive righteousness.[5]

Fourth, living by the Law does not produce righteousness in relation to others. If I am seeking to justify or prove myself, I will manipulate people to accomplish my justification. I am incapable of love, because I need to use or to oppose people in my project to prove myself. I will love other people for my sake rather than for their sake. Paul claims that his opponents in Galatia sought to circumcise the Galatians in order that they might "make a good impression in the flesh" (6:12) and "so they may boast in your flesh" (6:13). Furthermore, Paul says that the opponents courted the Galatians by threatening to exclude the Galatians if the Galatians did not follow the Law (4:17), thus manipulating the Galatians into doing their will out of fear of being rejected by them. Paul implies that his opponents needed the Galatians to approve of them so that the opponents could justify themselves before God and others (6:13).

Finally, life under law leads to a divided humanity. When people base their acceptability as human beings on human achievements (even on the good works of God's Law), then inevitably boasting results and there are factions. Before his encounter with Jesus, Paul's own success in the Law (1:14) led him to persecute people who did not follow the Law as he did. He vigorously "persecuted the church of God and tried to destroy it" (1:13). People who base their identity on being better than others, as Paul had done, are boastful and arrogant, which leads to quarrels, factions, divisions, rage, shunning, oppression, and domination (5:19–21). On the other side, people who do not measure up to others engage in competition, negative comparisons, self-deprecation, lack of appreciation for their own gifts, guilt, shame, jealousy, and envy (5:21, 26).

In Paul's view, God never intended for people to live by the Law in the first place. It is not as if God tried to get people to become righteous by the Law, but failed, and then sent Jesus to die so people's failures might be forgiven. On the contrary, Paul argues, God originally intended for people to relate to God based on faith in God's grace, freely, out of security, and from gratitude and love. God gave the promise to Abraham as a gift of grace. When, 430 years later, God gave the Law to Moses, the Law did not nullify the promise or add anything to it (3:15–18). God gave the Law only as a temporary measure until the promise to Abraham was fulfilled. The Law restrained transgressions "until the offspring should come to whom the promise had been made" (3:19). Jesus is the offspring who fulfilled the promise given to Abraham by grace, and now people, incorporated into Christ, could relate to God with faith in God's grace, just as Abraham did. Paul goes on to say that now "we are no longer under a guardian [that is, the Law]" (3:24). Thus, God never intended for works of the Law to be the basis of a relationship with God or to be the means for people to be righteous in relation to others.

For Paul, then, the human condition is self-justification evident in boasting and envy, which together result in a broken humanity. Paul knew from experience the evil that people do in the course of trying to prove how right they are and how important they are and how much better they (or their group) are than others. For Paul, people were meant to be reconciled in community in relation to God. In Christ, God provided the reconciliation that eliminated the need to prove anything and that enabled people to be at peace with God and in righteous relations with each other—Judeans and Gentiles alike.

The Vision for Human Life: Life in Response to Grace

Paul's vision for human life is that people will be entirely dependent on God's grace for their identity and their righteousness/ Justification, totally apart from Law. People are stripped of both successes and failures as they stand before God. "There is now no condemnation for those who are in Christ Jesus" (Romans 8:1). There is nothing of human effort that people can bring before God as grounds for God's acceptance. The matter is out of human hands. God has already justified people, and the appropriate human response is to accept that acceptance. As an analogy, consider a story from a leader at a retreat:

> My wife and I have a friend who was out to prove that no one could love him. He had a childhood full of rejection. One Christmas in his childhood, the grandparents who were raising him told him that if he did not lose a lot of weight by Christmas, there would be no presents. Sure enough, there was no Christmas that year for my friend. In his adult life, he was an engaging person, but he managed to do everything he could to alienate people who befriended him—unannounced visits, requests for difficult favors, staying too long, and so on. In order to remain his friend, we had to set limits on his intrusions. Yet he continued, in his quest to find love, to prove we could not love him. One day in exasperation, we said to him, "Look, we are

your friend because we have chosen to be your friend, so there's nothing you can do to make us your friends and nothing you can do to stop us from being your friends. So why don't you just relax and enjoy our friendship?"

Just so with God. God wishes to befriend us unconditionally as a commitment, as a gift. Just as some people cannot receive love because they know only rejection, others cannot accept love because they feel they must be worthy. We all know people who receive a gift and feel they do not deserve it; so they refuse to accept the gift or they immediately try to find a way to pay it back. They can only relate to others in terms of merit. But God wishes to give gifts—so why don't we just relax and accept them. God chooses to relate to people out of unconditional love. Therefore, to turn to Law as the Galatians have done, to seek to earn what God has already given, is, in Paul's view, to undermine the entire relationship God chooses to have with humanity—indeed, the only kind of relationship that can produce true righteousness.

For Paul, faith describes the proper human response to salvation as gift. Faith is the posture before God that receives grace and lives out of it. Faith is the ongoing dependence upon God as the ground and sustainer of physical, spiritual, and moral existence. Sometimes people will make faith into one more prerequisite, as if to substitute a mental act of belief for works of the Law as the basis whereby God will accept people—as though to say, "If we believe hard enough, then God will accept us." On the contrary, faith is the trust in God that implies *nothing in us* saves us, not even our "beliefs." God's grace saves people for a righteous life together, through faith, because faith is the receiving of, the trust in, and the dependency upon that grace. Justification and the Spirit are gifts freely given, and faith receives the gifts and allows them to be operative in life on an ongoing basis.

Faith is an entirely different way of being in the world. For Paul, receiving grace is totally opposite from earning justification by doing works of the Law. To take on the Law as a way to justify ourselves is to "drop out of grace" (5:4). It is to come under bondage to a "yoke of slavery" (5:2), for to be required to do something as a precondition for acceptance is to place oneself in a kind of slavery. For Gentiles to take on the Law is the same as if they had reverted to the slavery of adherence to idols (4:3, 9–10).

For Paul, the fall from grace is not a plunge into horrible sins but a decision to live by the Law as a means to justify ourselves before God! Paul says to those who seek to live by the Law that "Christ will be of no benefit to you" (5:1; 2:21). Paul asserts that those who want to be justified by works of the Law are "estranged from Christ" (5:4), that is, estranged from an orientation to grace. "For in Christ," Paul writes, "neither circumcision nor uncircumcision counts for anything but only faith active in love" (5:6).

This way of being in the world is a "new creation" (6:15). Jesus' death on the cross is the watershed that marks the end of one world and the beginning of a new creation. It is death to our old selves, because it makes a whole new life possible for humanity. As Paul says, "the world had been crucified to me and I to the world" (6:14). Everyone is to be seen in a new light. Paul says that he no longer judges anyone by human distinctions as a basis for acceptance or for relationships (see 2 Corinthians 5:16–17). Everyone is now perceived through the eyes of God's justification in Christ. All people are equally dependent on God for their acceptability as human beings.

The key is this: there is now no longer any reason for boasting or jealousy, no use for arrogance or self-deprecation, no grounds for racism or ethnocentricity, no need for quarrels and dissensions, no basis upon which to dominate or to be dominated. There is no longer place for division in the human community. All are equally dependent upon God for their justification as human beings. "What do you have that you have not received?" Paul asks (see 1 Corinthians 4:7). And if this is so, then there is every reason to live so as to build up the community rather than to tear it down. "If the Spirit is the source of our life," Paul writes, "let the Spirit also direct our course. Let us not become boastfully vain, provoking one another, envying one another" (5:25–26). If what we strive for is already provided, then there is no need to envy it in others or to acquire it at the expense of others. The human community now made possible by this new situation is truly a "new creation." For Paul, this *is* the beginning of salvation now, this rescue from the evil age for a restored creation. In a sense, people are called to live out the righteousness they have *already* acquired (5:16, 21).

In this transformed life, one is freed from the entire Law of

Moses as prerequisite, not only from the ritual laws, from circumcision and the celebration of seasons, but also from the moral laws. People have been called to freedom from all law as prerequisite for justification. Paul expresses this most starkly in 1 Corinthians when he writes, "Everything is permissible!" (1 Corinthians 6:12; 10:23). This is an astounding statement. It ends all specific moral laws and regulations. Because there are no prerequisites for acceptance, there are therefore no binding laws. People do not act to secure themselves or to prove anything. Their actions are an expression of what they have already become by virtue of what God has done in Christ. There is freedom, and no law is binding. Obviously, such an attitude on Paul's part has been the source of much misunderstanding, both in his time and in ours. What did he mean? Are people now free to do anything they please? Is everything really permissible?

We must listen carefully to Paul in order to understand him. Where there is no more Law, there are only two orientations: Spirit (God's work) or flesh (human effort)—a choice between life lived in response to God's Spirit or life lived on human terms apart from Spirit. Paul says that in life as response to Spirit, "Everything is permissible, but not everything is beneficial. Everything is permissible, but not everything builds up" (1 Corinthians 10:23). Only behavior that is consonant with the Spirit is beneficial, while behavior that comes out of human self-seeking is of no benefit. "One reaps whatever one sows. Whoever sows into the flesh will reap a harvest of corruption from the flesh, but whoever sows into the Spirit will reap a harvest of eternal life from the Spirit" (6:8). There are still consequences for immoral behavior, but they are not external punishments for transgressions of the Law. Rather, Spirit "produces" eternal life, and flesh "produces" corruption. Those actions that are consonant with the gift of the Spirit intrinsically bear life-giving fruit. Those actions that are not consonant with Spirit intrinsically produce death. As Paul says elsewhere, "The wages of sin is death, but the free gift of God is eternal life in Christ Jesus" (Romans 6:23). As such, there is only life lived in response to Spirit or there is death. For those who live by Spirit, "the fruit [not works!] of the Spirit is love, joy, peace, patience, kindness, goodness, faithfulness, humility, self-control" (5:22–23). Paul observes wryly that those who do such things can hardly be living under the Law of Moses, because there are no laws that prohibit such things! (5:23). Therefore, those who are led by the Spirit are not under Law (5:18).

So, then, what guides believers in this new life of grace? We can name three things. First, we are guided by what enables us to "continue in God's kindness" (Romans 11:22). Life lived out of grace is life lived in a gratitude that seeks to be worthy of all one has been given (Philippians 1:27). In Romans, Paul recounts at length all that God has done in Jesus, and then he adds: "*Therefore*, present your bodies, a living sacrifice, holy and acceptable to God, which is your reasonable service" (see Romans 12:1). Ethical behavior toward others is to be consistent with the self-giving way God has related to humans. Paul condemns Peter for "not acting consistently with the truth of the gospel" (2:14). Because God has acted to obliterate all human distinctions, therefore Peter should not make such human distinctions. As the Galatians seek to live in consonance with the Gospel, "Christ takes shape among" them (4:19).

Second, life lived out of grace is life lived in response to the Spirit. The Spirit is the power that effects righteousness. "If the Spirit is the source of our life," Paul says, "let the Spirit also direct our course" (5:25). Following this statement, Paul gives several examples of how members of the community should exercise the gentleness of Spirit—carry one another's burdens, bear their own burden for the benefit of the community, share all good things with each other, do good for all humanity, and do not grow weary of loving (6:1–10). In other words, the Spirit given freely out of God's love leads people to act in love for each other. Because the Spirit is present guiding and bearing fruit for the upbuilding of the community, there is no need for the Law. Why depend on secondary regulations when the reality of God's own living Spirit is present to give direct guidance?

Finally, Paul freely uses any guidelines that reflect God's grace and that mirror the leading of the Spirit—traditions, customs, words of the Lord, common lists of vices and virtues, Paul's own judgments in the Spirit, common sense, observations about creation, and so on. Thus, there is tremendous freedom in the way people live in response to grace. As Paul tells the Galatians, "For freedom Christ has set us free" (5:1) and, "You were called to freedom" (5:13). Almost never does Paul revert to the Law of Moses as a guideline for ethical judgments among these Gentiles, except when he writes: "The whole law is fulfilled in one word, 'You shall love your neighbor as yourself' " (5:14). This is not to resort to the Law as a way of life, but to show that God's intention behind the Law is available now directly through the Spirit apart from the Law of Moses. The principle underlying the life and impetus of the Spirit is that people are to love one another, to become servants of one another (5:13). Paul employs any guidelines that foster such a life.

The result of all God's activity is that genuine righteousness is now possible when before it was not possible. The whole point is that God's justification is the only way to produce a righteous world. In Greek, the word for "justification" was also the word for "righteousness." Where God has now provided justification, there also God has made righteousness possible. For example, the righteousness of genuine love is now possible. Because one is already justified, there is no need to manipulate others in order to get approval or reassurance for oneself. Therefore one can love for the sake of the other, just as God loves. As Paul writes elsewhere, "Love is patient and kind, love is not jealous or boastful, love is not arrogant or rude, love does not insist on its own way. . ." (1 Corinthians 13). Such love creates a new world, a world of righteousness.

In summary, Paul has a thoroughgoing understanding of justification at all levels. He showed in his letter how individuals by their faith in God's grace stand justified before God; he gave extensive directions for communal relations in light of the grace of Christ (5:16–6:10); and he envisioned worldwide reconciliation among the major social, economic, religious, and gender divisions of the ancient world. The Christian community *is* the new humanity in Christ: "Everyone who has been baptized into Christ has put on Christ, for in Christ there is neither Judean nor Greek, neither slave nor free, no male and female, for you are all one in Christ Jesus" (3:26–28). This is Paul's comprehensive vision of reconciliation within which the individual, the community, and all humanity are transformed for a life of righteousness.

The Transformation: Grace as the Means to Righteousness

How does God save people from the human condition for a life of grace, from a life of division and strife to a life of righteousness and justice? The key to Paul's understanding is that the death of Jesus on the cross freed people from the curse associated with trying to live up to the Law and granted people a new and different relationship with God and with other people. Paul is not precisely clear how Jesus' death effects justification. Paul knows from Jesus' resurrection that the curse he bore in his death on the tree must not have been his own curse, for the resurrection confirmed his innocence. Jesus must have died for the sin of others. However, in Paul's view, Jesus did not die as an atonement for sins to be forgiven. Rather, Jesus died so as to "rescue us from the present evil age" (1:4). A curse of punishment was associated with the restraint offered by the Law. Because people disobeyed, all were under a curse in relation to the Law; yet "Christ redeemed us from the curse of the law by becoming a curse for us. As it is written, 'Cursed is everyone who hangs upon a tree' " (3:13). In a representative way, Jesus took upon himself the curse of the Law that was on others. Thus, Jesus did not die for *sins*; rather, Jesus stood in for humanity in some representative way to remove the curse.

As such, Jesus' death involved the abolition of the Law as the way to acceptance before God. There are two ways to deal with sin as transgression against the Law. The first way is to offer forgiveness where people fail. The second way is to remove the law! Where there is no law, sin is not reckoned as transgression (2:18; see Romans 4:15; 5:13). In Paul's view, baptism does not mean forgiveness, but death and resurrection. By baptism, people have died with Christ, and therefore the Law no longer applies to them! In relation to his own life, Paul writes, "Through law, I died to law so that I might live for God. I have been crucified with Christ, so that it is no longer I who live but Christ lives in me" (3:19). At the end of the letter, Paul writes that through the cross "the world has been crucified to me and I to the world" (6:14). As a result, Paul now lives by faith in the Son of God "who loved me and gave himself up [to death] for me" (3:20; 1:4). Since the curse was removed and since Law is no longer in effect, people now stand righteous, justified before God.

Justification is so powerful because it deals with the whole person before God. Forgiveness deals only with our guilt, whereas justification deals also with our shame. The following illustration may help to explain.

> A spiritual director once recommended to a group that we list all the things of which we might be ashamed—not just actions or feelings for which we feel guilty, but also our limitations, our disabilities, our appearance, our habits, our unacceptability to others—and in regard to each thing to offer this affirmation: "This thing of which I am ashamed does not keep me from being justified as a human being before God, because we are justified by grace." Next we listed all the things of which we were proud—skills, capabilities, appearance, achievements—and then in regard to each thing to affirm: "This thing of which I am proud does not justify me as a human being before God, because we are justified by grace."

Thus, justification affirms the whole human being both in terms of guilt *and* in terms of shame.

Such deep affirmation creates a solid place on which to stand in *solid-arity* with each other.

> In a heated discussion among a diversity of people in a seminary, comments were made to suggest that all whites are racist and all men are sexist. Some in the group were angry and defiant while others were fearful and defensive. Finally a black woman broke the tension when she said, "Look, we're all sitting here wondering if there is anything redeeming about me, anything worth loving about me. If I could just prove my decency to you, I would have a place on which to stand. But it's not about being good or bad. We're all accepted by God. So just tell us that you stand with us now and we'll struggle together."

This woman knew that although we can sometimes feel united by the fact that we are all good or that we are all sinners, the ultimate basis for solidarity among all of us comes from outside of us, in the acceptance of us by God. Unconditional justification from God reconciles divisions and gives us a solid place on which to stand together—across genders, races, nations, and cultures—despite our moral rightness or our pain and our complicity in sin.

God's act in Jesus is truly one of grace from the divine side. Regarding Paul's thought, we may erroneously think of Jesus' death in the following way: God was angry with people because of their sins, and in order to appease God's wrath Jesus had to provide a sacrifice adequate to satisfy God so that God would then be willing to accept human beings and make available the Spirit. In this later (medieval) view of the atonement, God is the one who needs to be reconciled to people, as if God were an offended party concerned mainly for God's self. But in Paul's view, the problem lies not with God but with humanity. Humanity is under the curse of the Law, and this situation has made people enemies of God. God removes the barrier to God by removing the Law as well as the curse that resulted from people disobeying the Law. Human beings no longer have to strive to please God in order to be justified and no longer need to resent God as an enemy because they are unable to live up to standards God has set (see Romans 5:10). Thus, God was in Christ *not in order to reconcile God's self to the world*. Rather, "God was in Christ *reconciling the world to God's self*" (2 Corinthians 5:18–19). The act of God was an act of grace, done not to satisfy God but for the sake of humanity.

The event of justification is thus an empowering event of grace. While demands on people as a prerequisite for acceptance do not and cannot produce righteousness, grace can. Grace alone can lead one to praise God for God's sake and love others for their sake. From beginning to end, Paul portrays the whole relationship of God with people as one of empowering grace—from the promise for Abraham to God's act on the cross to the gift of the Spirit to the life and ethical fruit of the Spirit. Also, Paul's role as an apostle originates from grace. God called Paul "by his grace" (1:15). Paul does not first try to convince people of their sinfulness or establish prerequisites or threaten rejection. Paul argues that there is no manipulative "persuasion" to his proclamation (1:10; 5:8). It is pure announcement of grace (see 2 Corinthians 5:18–19). Finally, Paul's letter itself is an event of grace. Paul does not restore the Galatian people by first convicting them of their sin, then having them confess their sin, and finally offering them forgiveness. Rather, he re-preaches the gospel of grace, chiding them for their foolishness in abandoning that gospel (3:1–5) and drawing them again into the orbit of God's grace. He expresses his confidence that "they will take no other view" (5:10). Paul begins and ends the letter expressing his desire that "grace" be with the Galatians (1:3; 6:18). Thus, the proclaiming word of Paul's letter itself bears the transformation from this evil age to the new creation, a new creation in which life is given and received and lived as grace.

Pauline/Galatians Trajectories

Some years ago, a survey asked selected history professors from around the United States who they thought were the most influential people in Western civilization. Both Jesus and Paul ranked near the top, but Paul ranked ahead of Jesus! Through his missionary activity, Paul was a dominant influence in the spread of Christianity throughout the Roman world. However, the distinctive "theological" influence of Paul was not felt in a significant way until the time of Augustine in the fourth century, whose understanding of sin and whose articulation of God's love reflected the views of Paul. Later, Paul's theology was a driving force behind the Protestant Reformation of the sixteenth century. The belief in justification by faith has shaped many Protestant denominations, particularly in terms of the theology of salvation by grace—which is the source of much great preaching among Baptist, Presbyterian, Methodist, Lutheran, Discipleship traditions, and other denominations. Central to African American preaching across many denominations has been the Pauline conviction that God is impartial, that God neither favors some nations and people nor discriminates against other people and nations.

Today, many groups turn to Galatians for strength and formation in their Christian lives, often for different reasons. Not only Lutherans, but many Evangelical Christians in general find the emphasis on the gospel of grace to be a rallying point for the Christian life. Paul's vision in Galatians of reconciliation and equality among social groups, races, and sexes has shaped much of the church's quest to eliminate discrimination of all kinds. African Americans find in Galatians a ringing declaration of freedom. Many groups of Christian women and men turn to Galatians for the primary vision of "no male and female" in Christ for equality among the genders. Also, Paul's rejection of law and his emphasis on the Spirit as the source of morality have been key ingredients in the development of "situation ethics" in many Christian circles.

Example of a Pauline Community

An imaginary example of a contemporary community shaped by Paul's vision for the church would be rooted thoroughly in the unconditional acceptance by God for all. Preaching, worship, and decision making would reinforce the proclamation of God's grace and reflect the spontaneity and freedom of Paul's gospel. Every week would be thanksgiving. The educational program would avoid moralizing and foster responsible relationships rooted in love. The community would be inclusive and organized for a ministry of mutuality. People would be accepting of one another, free to acknowledge weaknesses, eager to listen to each other, and able to encourage each other without recrimination. Visitors would experience not simply friendliness, but unconditional acceptance. The worship patterns, manner of decision making, structure, and educational program would reflect the strengths and needs of the diverse ethnic, racial, and gender groups that comprised the community. Conflicts and difficulties would be overcome in a positive way by seeking to restore an orientation to grace. The mission of the community would be to create right-eousness in society, and it would include a strong commitment to overcome all forms of discrimination. The community might see itself as an experiment in grace where God's vision for humanity was being lived now.

Notes

1. Scholars generally consider that Paul wrote Romans, 1 and 2 Corinthians, Galatians, 1 Thessalonians, Philippians, and Philemon. Other letters attributed to Paul were probably written by followers of Paul after his death: Colossians, Ephesians, 2 Thessalonians, 1 and 2 Timothy, and Titus.

2. A theology of justification does not appear explicitly in the rest of Paul's authentic letters. Paul's letters, taken together, constitute a minor canon-of-diversity in their own right, for Paul did not have a generic theology for all circumstances and places. Rather, it seems likely that after Paul had announced in a particular location God's offer of salvation apart from the Law of Israel, he went on to theologize contextually in relation to that local culture. Therefore, in his letter to the Philippians, Paul uses metaphors of citizenship and military battles to address Christians in a city that served as a Roman colony for retired soldiers. In his letter to the Thessalonians, Paul draws on local experiences of Greco-Roman philosophical schools and itinerant teachers as the means to clarify his relationship with them. Writing to the wealthy Philemon, Paul uses the models of patron-client interactions and household relationships to exact a favorable decision from Philemon on behalf of Onesimus.

In 1 Corinthians, Paul employs metaphors from the culture used by others for overcoming civil strife, and he develops a theology of the cross to show the Corinthians how to reverse the factionalism in their community. In all of these examples, Paul draws upon, transforms, or counters the local cultural experiences of his audience in order to get across the Christian message. Thus, we are treating justification as only one of many theological perspectives present among the different Pauline letters.

3. The translation of Galatians in this chapter is based on the translation in the commentary by Hans Dieter Betz.

4. It is misleading to think that Judeans in general embraced the point of view that one has to carry out the Law completely. Also, it may be incorrect even to assume that Paul's Judean Christian opponents held this view. They might well have agreed with Paul that salvation comes through Jesus and not by Law but disagreed with Paul by saying that Gentiles are still called to follow the Law of Israel as an expression of the Christian life. However, Paul portrays the choice between Law and grace as mutually exclusive, probably because he thought that Gentiles would only embrace the Law as a prerequisite and that such an attitude would undermine the freedom of the gospel. Paul's depiction of opponents does not convey the life-giving role of Law as guide for life among Judeans of his day.

5. Elsewhere, Paul goes so far as to argue that the Law even stirs up the desire to do that which it prohibits and thereby creates an even greater tendency to sin (Romans 7:7–25). Thus, human life apart from God (which Paul calls "flesh") uses Law in opposition to Spirit and leads people to "do the very things which they do not intend" (Galatians 5:16–18).

Further Reading

Achtemeier, P. J. *The Quest for Unity in the New Testament Church: A Study in Paul and Acts*. Philadelphia: Fortress Press, 1987.

Altmann, Walter. *Luther and Liberation*. Minneapolis: Fortress Press, 1993.

Balmer, Randall. *Mine Eyes Have Seen the Glory: A Journey into the Evangelical Subculture of America*. Oxford: Oxford University Press, 1989.

Barrett, C. K. *Freedom and Obligation: A Study of the Epistle to the Galatians*. Philadelphia: Westminster, 1985.

Betz, H. D. *Galatians: A Commentary on Paul's Letter to the Churches in Galatia*. Philadelphia: Fortress Press, 1979.

Braaten, Carl. *Justification: The Article by Which the Church Stands or Falls*. Minneapolis: Fortress Press, 1990.

Campbell, William. *Paul's Gospel in an Intercultural Context: Jew and Gentile in the Letter to the Romans*. Frankfurt: Peter Lang, 1991.

Davies, W. D. *Paul and Rabbinic Judaism*. London: SPCK, 1955.

Elliott, Neil. *Liberating Paul: The Justice of God and the Politics of the Apostle*. Maryknoll: Orbis, 1994.

Felder, Cain Hope. *Troubling Biblical Waters: Race, Class, and Family.* Maryknoll: Orbis, 1989.

Fiorenza, Elisabeth Schüssler. *In Memory of Her: A Feminist Theological Reconstruction of Christian Origins.* New York: Crossroad, 1985.

Fletcher, Joseph. *Situation Ethics: The New Morality.* Philadelphia: Westminster, 1966.

Fung, R. Y. K. *The Epistle to the Galatians.* Grand Rapids: Eerdmans, 1988.

Furnish, V. P. *The Moral Teaching of Paul.* 2d edition. Nashville: Abingdon, 1979.

Hall, Sidney. *Christian Anti-Semitism and Paul's Theology.* Minneapolis: Fortress Press, 1993.

Krentz, Edgar. *Galatians.* Minneapolis: Augsburg, 1985.

Matera, Frank. *Galatians.* Collegeville, Minn.: The Liturgical Press, 1992.

Neyrey, Jerome. *Paul, In Other Words: A Cultural Reading of His Letters.* Louisville: Westminster/John Knox, 1990.

Osiek, Carolyn. *Galatians.* Wilmington, Del.: Michael Glazier, 1980.

Roetzel, C. J. *The Letters of Paul: Conversations in Context.* Atlanta: John Knox, 1982.

Russell, Letty, editor. *Feminist Interpretation of the Bible,* especially chapter 4. Philadelphia: Westminster, 1985.

Sanders, E. P. *Paul.* Oxford: Oxford University Press, 1991.

Scroggs, R. *Paul for a New Day.* Philadelphia: Fortress Press, 1977.

Segundo, Juan Luis. *The Humanist Christology of Paul.* Maryknoll: Orbis, 1986.

Stendahl, K. *Paul Among Jews and Gentiles.* Philadelphia: Fortress Press, 1976.

Tamez, Elsa. *The Amnesty of Grace: Justification by Faith from a Latin American Perspective,* translated by Sharon Ringe. Nashville: Abingdon, 1993.

3
The Gospel of Mark
Courage in the Face of Death

Background and Purpose

WHILE PAUL'S LETTER REFERS ONLY TO THE DEATH and resurrection of Jesus, the Gospels portray also the public ministry of Jesus. Mark's Gospel was the first Gospel and was probably written some fifteen to twenty years after Galatians, under different historical circumstances and in a different geographical locale. Scholars are not sure who wrote the Gospel of Mark. Some traditions in the later church attributed this Gospel to a certain interpreter of Peter named "Mark" (1 Peter 5:13), who "wrote down the memoirs of Peter but not in the right order." Yet, based on the source of the tradition and the Gospel itself, there are good reasons to doubt this tradition. For convenience, we will nevertheless refer to the author as Mark.

Despite uncertainty about the person of the author, we may nevertheless infer a great deal about the author from the story of Mark itself. Mark's Gospel appears to have been composed from a peasant perspective, probably for Judeans and Gentiles in the regions of northern Palestine around Galilee or Syria, as a way to urge the spreading of the good news about the kingdom of God before the end came and Jesus returned in glory. The Gospel of Mark was probably written during or just after the Roman-Judean War of 66 to 70 C.E.[1] In that war, Israel revolted against the Roman overlords. The Romans defeated the Judeans, conquered Jerusalem, and destroyed the Temple. Mark wrote about Jesus, in part, in order to show that any attempt to dominate others by force—by Israel or by Rome—was contrary to God's way of ruling over the world.

Mark's Gospel announces that Jesus inaugurated God's rule on earth, a realm that brings life rather than destruction, a realm that fosters service rather than domination. As Mark tells it, Jesus demonstrated the presence of God's rulership through such acts as healings, exorcisms, authority over nature, the provision of abundant bread in the desert, and prophetic confrontations with the authorities. In Mark, Jesus calls disciples to announce this realm of God to the world. Mark believed that Jesus' return and the final establishment of God's kingdom were imminent. He therefore enjoined urgency and alertness in the mission of spreading the news of God's kingdom to all the nations before the end came.

It is generally accepted that Mark wrote to followers who faced persecution in their mission to proclaim the good news. The time of the Roman-Judean War was difficult for followers of Jesus. On the one hand, they were the target of opposition from some other Judeans, because they opposed the war. On the other hand, they were suspected by Gentiles because their leader had been executed as a Judean revolutionary. They faced ridicule, rejection, ostracism from family and community, betrayal, arrests, trials, floggings, and death (13:5–23). It was threatening even to admit an association with Jesus, let alone to proclaim the good news of the kingdom (14:66–72; 16:1–8).

Although followers of Jesus undoubtedly knew courage, they must often have failed to speak or to act for the good news because of their fear. Mark addressed this situation of persecution and fear. Mark's narrative led hearers of his Gospel to face the fear of persecution and empowered them to spread the good news faithfully and courageously. The depiction of Jesus' loyalty to his stumbling and fearful disciples encouraged readers to spread the good news despite past failures and ongoing persecution.

Discerning the standards of judgment that govern a narrative like the Gospel of Mark is different from discerning the standards of judgment in a letter like Galatians. The standards of judgment in a narrative are those values and beliefs embedded in the story by which the readers are led to evaluate the characters and events in a story. In a letter, the standards of judgment are explicitly stated by the author in addressing the readers. In a Gospel, the standards of judgment are implicit and indirect. The narrator does not "tell" us directly what these standards are. Rather, the narrator "shows" us the standards indirectly through the depictions of the characters and in the descriptions of events. We therefore infer the two ways from features of Mark's narrative such as the evaluative comments of the narrator, the teachings of Jesus, the actions and fate of the characters, the words of God, quotations from scripture, and so on. From these we can see the positive standards that the narrative promotes as well as the negative standards that the narrative condemns. Highlighting the positive as well as the negative standards shows us both sides of the same coin, for Mark's narrative condemns behavior that is the opposite of the behavior it fosters. [2]

The Two Ways: "Saving" One's Life out of Fear or "Losing" One's Life for Others

The Gospel of Mark is a tightly woven narrative reflecting two contrasting ways of living. At one point in the narrative, Jesus rebukes Peter, saying, "Get behind me Satan, because you are not thinking the things of God but human things" (8:33). Here is a contrast between two sets of values, two orientations to life: (1) the things of God, that is, what God wills people to be and (2) the things of humans, that is, what people want for themselves (what people in their fear and blindness think is best for themselves).

The Markan Jesus states these contrasting standards at the beginning of the journey to Jerusalem (8:22–10:52). Then, in teaching his disciples on the way to Jerusalem, Jesus elaborates what God wants for people. The disciples resist Jesus at every point because they selfishly want what people want for themselves. So the journey becomes a clash of values between Jesus who teaches what God wills for people and the disciples who exemplify what people want for themselves. On the way, Jesus predicts three times to the disciples his impending persecution and death (8:31–9:1; 9:30–50; 10:32–45). After each prediction, the disciples show that they do not understand or accept his teachings. After each of these reactions, Jesus in turn explains to his disciples the values of the rule of God that underlie his words and actions.

The teachings that come after these three predictions on the way to Jerusalem are the core standards of Mark's Gospel. After the first prediction, Jesus says, "Those who want to save their lives will lose them, but those who will lose their lives for me and the good news will save them" (8:35). After the second prediction, Jesus teaches, "If anyone wants to be most important, that person will be least of all and a servant of all" (9:35). After the third prediction, Jesus says, "Whoever wants to be great among you will be your servant, and whoever wants to be most important will be everyone's slave. For even the son of humanity came not to be served, but to serve and to give his life a ransom for many" (10:43–45).

Each of these three teachings involves a contrast between acquisition (saving one's life) and relinquishment (losing one's life for the good news). People who follow the world's standards seek to acquire and maintain status and power for themselves. This way of life is motivated by fear. By contrast, people who follow Jesus' standards welcome the blessings of the kingdom and are willing to relinquish life, status, and power in order to bring the good news of this kingdom. This way of life is a way of courage made possible by faith. Thus, for Mark, the two ways of life are "saving one's life out of fear" or "losing one's life for the good news out of faith." Here are the characteristic Markan standards of these two ways.

What people want out of fear	*What God wants for people*
Be self-centered	Be other-centered for God
Be blind to the rule of God	See the rule of God
Oppose the kingdom	Receive the kingdom's blessings
Save one's own life	Lose one's life for the good news
Acquire the world	Give up possessions for the poor
Be great	Be least in relation to others
Lord over others	Be servant to all
Be anxious	Have faith, trust
Have fear	Have courage
Harm others	Save others
Be loyal to self alone	Be loyal to God for others

Mark's narrative consistently promotes the one way and condemns the other way. As such, the characters in Mark's narrative embody one or the other of these two ways. Jesus embodies "what God wills for people." He heals, drives out demons, pardons sins, feeds hungry people, confronts oppressors, and dies as a result of being persecuted for this mission. Also, the minor characters who come to Jesus for healing often exemplify "the things of God." They have faith and are willing to serve and to be least. By contrast, the authorities embody "what people want for themselves," for they aggrandize themselves at the expense of others. They are afraid and seek to save their honor and to maintain their positions of power. Finally, the disciples vacillate between the two ways. They are torn between following Jesus in service to the good news and following Jesus in order to acquire status and power for themselves. In these characterizations, Mark promotes the values and beliefs of the kingdom by positive example, and Mark rejects the opposite values and beliefs by negative example. Mark means to persuade readers to embrace values that will create a society of mutual service, free of oppression.

The Human Condition: The Fearful Saving of Self

The negative standards of the Gospel of Mark reflect Mark's view of human sinfulness, namely, that people are self-oriented and self-serving. People want to "save their lives" (8:35), to "acquire the world" (8:36), to "be great" (9:35), and to "lord it over" others (10:42–44).

According to Mark, the authorities in Israel exemplify this way of life. They have status, power, and security, and they are bent on maintaining them. They have taken control of the vineyard of Israel for themselves and do not bear the fruit on behalf of Israel's people that God requires of them (12:1–12). They love their importance and they abuse their power: they love to be greeted in the markets; they want the best seats in the synagogue and at the banquets; and they devour the houses of widows (12:38–40). At the crucifixion, they ridicule Jesus because he "cannot save himself" (15:31).

For Mark, the quest to maintain power and status is motivated by fear (11:18). In the Markan portrayals, the Judean and Gentile authorities are afraid. Herod fears John the Baptist (6:20). Pilate defers to the crowd (15:15). The Judean authorities fear Jesus' popularity (15:10). They fear losing their position as a result of Jesus' activity (12:7), and they fear losing face with the crowds (6:26; 12:12). Such fear is the opposite of faith/trust in God, which brings courage in the face of threat and loss.

For fear of losing their power and status, the leaders destroy others. Although Herod considers John the Baptist to be a right-eous man, he nevertheless executes John because he does not want to break his oath to Herodias's daughter—for fear of losing face before "the most important" and "the greatest" people of Galilee (6:26). Although Pilate thinks that Jesus is innocent and knows that the high priests have handed him over out of envy, he nevertheless executes Jesus in order to "do the satisfactory thing" for the crowd (15:15). Also, out of envy, the Judean leaders seek to trap, discredit, and destroy Jesus. They bend the law, arrest Jesus surreptitiously (14:7), suborn witnesses (14:55), hold a kangaroo court (15:3), and stir up the crowd to release Barabbas (15:11)—all in order to maintain their status and preserve their authority over the people.

The disciples often reflect the same values as the authorities. Although the disciples leave all to follow Jesus, they desire to acquire status and power from Jesus. Early on, the disciples are enamored with the crowds (1:37). On the journey to Jerusalem, they argue about who is greatest among them (9:33–34). James and John ask if they can sit on the right and left of Jesus in his glory in the age to come (10:35–40). When the other ten disciples find out about this, they are angry (10:41). The disciples had hoped to gain glory and power from following Jesus.

So, too, the disciples are fearful. They are afraid in the storm on the lake (4:40). They are anxious about how to feed people in the desert (6:34–37; 8:4). They are afraid to ask Jesus about his death (9:34). They betray, flee, or deny Jesus, all in order to save themselves. Fear for themselves underlies their resistance to understanding, their lack of faith, and their failure to be faithful to the end.

In their fearful quest to acquire power and status, the disciples harm others and generate dissension. They argue with each other about who is greatest (9:33, 10:41); they stop an exorcist from driving out demons in Jesus' name (9:38); they rebuke the people who bring little children to Jesus for a blessing (10:13); and they vie for honors from Jesus (10:35–45). In response to Jesus' predictions of death, they seek to secure themselves. In so doing, they become elitist, exclusive, competitive, and domineering.

The disciples have bought into the values of their culture. The disciples do not have the power and honor that the authorities have, but they want them and they strive to attain them. We contemporary readers can identify with the longings of the disciples and the behavior that results. Both the opponents and the disciples of Mark's Gospel embrace the very values that also seem natural to our own culture. We want to be important and to receive recognition for it. We want to have positions of power in life to control how our lives will turn out, and we view our lives as a journey toward greater and greater financial security. The quest for status, power, and security is reflected in our culture, sometimes crassly, in such slogans as "looking out for number one," "getting ahead," "climbing to the top," and so on. So whether we have these things or are striving to attain them, they can define our lives. And just as the disciples seek to attain status and power from their relationship with Jesus, Christians in the United States often view a relationship with Jesus as the best way to attain success and wealth.

We can also identify with the fears of the disciples. The treatment of the disciples is no caricature that applies only to the lives of others. Like the disciples, some contemporary Christians do indeed face serious consequences for the convictions and actions that they take as Christians. That is not the case for most of us. However, even if we do not face persecution and death, we should not dismiss Mark's portrayal as applying only to people in extreme circumstances. Any loss of status or possessions or power is a form of death. When we are embarrassed we say, "I thought I'd die." When we experience rejection we say, "They treated me as if I didn't exist." When we encounter financial threat or loss we say, "I'm finished." These are death-like experiences of loss in everyday life. So when we fail to say what we believe for fear of embarrassment, when we fail to act against injustice for fear of rejection, when we fail to give generously to others for fear of our own loss of security, we are like the disciples of Jesus in Mark's story—who avoided living the good news because they wanted to avoid threats to their own security. We tend to limit our life as Christians to those words and actions that are safe, to what does not threaten our position or security. Perhaps if we acted for the kingdom in the radical ways Mark proposes, we too might be risking livelihood or the censure of the community or ostracism.

Mark's Gospel condemns the self-oriented, fear-filled quest for security, status, and power as contrary to what God wants people to be. In Mark's perspective, people who embrace these standards are destructive to others and ultimately to themselves. The result is a society of conflict and oppression. In Mark's view, the ultimate consequence of a destructive life is God's judgment against them (9:42–48; 12:40; 14:62).

The Vision for Human Life: The Courage to Live for Others

Characters who live the standards of the rule of God are willing to "lose their lives for Jesus and the good news" (8:35), to "be least of all and a servant of all" (9:35), and to "be everyone's slave" (10:43–45). These metaphors of service represent what God wills for people. While the Judean leaders, in Mark's portrayal, think that acquiring status and power over others is what makes people great, by contrast Jesus considers that the truly great human being gives up status and power on behalf of those with less power and status.

In Mark, Jesus lifts up certain metaphors as paradigms of these standards. The metaphor for being least is a child or a servant (9:35–37). The metaphor for the right use of power is a servant or slave (10:44), because the role of "slave" exists to benefit others and offers no opportunity to use power over others for self-aggrandizement. Jesus' models of greatness and service are a contrast to the leaders of the Gentile nations who lord over people (10:42–43). The values of the kingdom turn the world upside down, so that the roles on the bottom become the moral paradigms for all human relations. Jesus does not offer these models to people who are already forced to serve or be least—slaves or women or children. Rather, Jesus commends these models of relinquishment to people who already have status and power and who want to maintain them (the authorities) or to people who do not have status or power but who want to acquire them for themselves (the disciples). Jesus clearly opposes particular oppressors, but the key is that he opposes oppression as such. He means to stop the cycle of oppression and reverse it with a cycle of service.

Minor characters also embody the positive standards of judgment. Suppliants serve by bringing others for healing (2:3; 7:32; 8:22) or by coming on behalf of a relative (5:23; 7:26). The Syrophoenician woman accepts Jesus' designation of her as a little dog in order to get her daughter healed (7:28). The poor widow gives "her whole living" by giving out of her lack rather than out of her surplus. (12:41–44). An unnamed woman uses expensive ointment to anoint Jesus ahead of time for the burial (14:3–9). Joseph of Arimathea takes courage and approaches Pilate in order to give Jesus a burial before the Sabbath (15:43). Women go to anoint Jesus' body at the grave (16:1–3).

Despite their obvious failings as followers of Jesus, the disciples in Mark also sometimes exemplify the standards of the kingdom. They leave their homes, families, and occupations to follow Jesus in the service of the good news (1:14–20; 10:28–29). They serve Jesus in many ways: they protect him from the crowds (3:9), provide a boat for him (4:1), distribute food in the desert (6:34–44; 8:1–10), get a donkey (11:1–8), and prepare the Passover meal (14:12–16). Also, as "fishers for people" (1:17), they go from village to village without money, food, or extra clothes in order to drive out demons and anoint the sick for healing (6:7–13). They continue to follow Jesus until confronted with death.

For Mark, Jesus is the primary exemplar of the standards of the kingdom. He serves people in his healings, his exorcisms, his pardoning, his feedings, and his preaching without seeking acclamation for himself (see 1:43; 5:34). He speaks the truth of God whether people favor him or reject him (12:14). He refuses to lord it over others. As a result, he is persecuted by those whom he condemns. In his execution, Jesus manifests the standards of the rule of God in a dramatic way (15:1–37): He is least in the society as a human being ridiculed and rejected; he has relinquished power over anyone; and he loses his life in the service of bringing good news to the world. At Gethsemane, although Jesus is afraid to die, his prayer reveals the orientation of his life: "Abba, Father . . . not what *I want* but what *you want*" (14:36). Jesus is the opposite of self-oriented. He is God-centered for others.

For Mark, God wills that people receive all the blessings of the kingdom. Yet God also wills for people to endure loss and persecution for the mission of the kingdom. This Markan view of suffering calls for clarification. First, Mark does not value suffering or loss for its own sake. Rather, Jesus tells his disciples to pray that persecution not come (14:38). Second, in Mark's narrative, God does not will for humans to suffer illness, disability, demonic possession, or the destructive forces of nature. The extensive

Markan healings, exorcisms, and nature miracles demonstrate this. Therefore, when Jesus calls people to "take up their cross and follow me" (8:34), Jesus is not referring to suffering that comes from nonhuman forces, such as demons, illness, or nature.

Nor does God call people to suffer on behalf of those who are in a position of power over them. Jesus does not tell slaves that enforced service is among the standards of the rule of God. Hence, for example, Jesus would not call for a wife to endure abuse to serve the needs of her husband nor for a child to endure abuse to serve the needs of the parent. Quite the contrary; God wills to relieve all oppression by humans over other humans. In Mark, Jesus confronts and condemns such human oppression where he encounters it. In fact, it is precisely his opposition to human oppression that results in the persecution of him.

The "cross" of suffering that God does call people to endure is the loss and tragic persecution that come to followers in the course of living and proclaiming faithfully the good news of God's realm of salvation. Proclaiming the good news leads to encounters with those who oppress. However, in Mark, God does not give agents of the kingdom the right to use force to stop those who oppress; otherwise, they themselves would become oppressors over those whom they condemn. As a result, the followers of Jesus who confront oppression end up undergoing persecution at the hands of the very oppressors they condemn, just as Jesus did. In Mark, this suffering by persecution in the course of proclaiming the good news is "the cross" that God calls people to bear for the sake of the world, a cross people take up because they have chosen to live for the Gospel.

Thus, the Markan Jesus calls disciples to lose their lives "for me and the good news." Those who have status and exercise power at the expense of others are to relinquish them. Those who do not have status and power over others are not to seek them for themselves. If people already have status and power or if they acquire them, they are to use them not to aggrandize themselves but to empower others who are oppressed. We need to distinguish between what God is calling us to give up and what God is calling us to become. We are called to give up the self-serving values of the dominant culture, and we are called to true status and power in the service of God's realm. The new life in the kingdom calls for a new definition of greatness and power in which both status and authority are used and shared and, when necessary, risked in the course of serving the larger human community.

Thus, we are called to embrace the life-giving values of the kingdom and actively to oppose oppression in the course of bringing the good news. Because of the nature of the good news and because of the way the world is, people who offer good news to others will be risking their status, power, and life. Followers who are not prepared for such risks will shrink in fear and avoidance. A contemporary parallel to Mark's situation may help to clarify.

> In the late 1980s, a volunteer approached a leader of the Sanctuary Movement in the United States serving refugees from Central America, and she asked to join in the work of the movement.
> The leader said to her, "Before you say whether you really wish to join us, let me pose some questions: Are you ready to have your telephone tapped by the government? Are you prepared to have your neighbors shun you? Are you strong enough to have your children ridiculed and harassed at school? Are you ready to be arrested and tried, with full media coverage? If you are not prepared for these things, you may not be ready to join the movement. For when push comes to shove, if you fear these things, you will not be ready to do what needs to be done for the refugees."
> The woman decided to think it over.

Similarly, if followers of Jesus are not ready to give up their status and their power over others, then they will not be ready to proclaim the good news. Mark's Gospel leads people to confront their fear and to accept the persecution that may come in the course of following Jesus. Mark's narrative calls people to celebrate life and oppose oppression in spite of the risks.

For Mark, living the standards of the kingdom is possible by faith, by trusting God. The total response to the arrival of the kingdom, rightly understood, is to have "faith in the good news" of the kingdom (1:13). The arrival of the power of the kingdom in the person of Jesus awakens faith and makes faith possible. Faith is trust in the God for whom all is possible—the God who heals, drives out demons, calms storms, provides bread in the desert, and raises one to life and salvation in the new age. This faith gives courage, for faith is the opposite of fear (4:40; 5:36; 6:50). When we can ultimately count on God for life, we have the courage to risk life for others (10:21). In Mark, the faith that one's future salvation is in God's care gives one neither complacency nor passive security but the courage to risk even persecution, to live a life of abandon for the good news (10:29–30; 14:36).

The narrative calls followers of Jesus to have faith in God as Jesus had faith in God, the faith that enabled Jesus to keep on living for the kingdom even though it led to his execution (8:34). With his story of Jesus, Mark seeks to turn the culture around from a society that is destructive to one that promotes life. The ultimate consequences of living the standards of the kingdom are resurrection and eternal life in the age to come (10:30).

The Transformation: New Life, Sight, and Empowerment in the Face of Death

How do we reverse oppression and create a world of mutual service? How are people empowered to relinquish the values of the world and embrace the standards of the kingdom? How do self-oriented people become God-centered in service to others? For Mark, this transformation involves three dynamics: first, *receiving* the gift of God's rule with all its blessings; second, *seeing* how to live life in a new way; and, finally, *being empowered* to live for others on behalf of the good news.

First, like the people in the story, the readers of Mark are invited to receive the kingdom, for "Unless you receive the rule of God as a little child [receives things], you definitely will not enter into it" (10:15). The entire story of Mark is the display of this kingdom that brings liberation from all forms of oppression. Jesus heals the sick, drives out demons, pardons sins, cleanses lepers, restores the disabled, delivers from the threats of nature, welcomes the outcast, challenges inhumane laws, calls the wealthy to give to the poor, confronts fraud and extortion in the Temple, and calls the leaders of Israel to produce the fruits of the vineyard. Out of compassion, the Markan Jesus offers the power of the kingdom to restore people to physical and moral wholeness. Receiving and entering this realm of God is a matter of having faith that life, now and in the future, comes from God. Living by this kingdom is nothing less than a Copernican-like revolution from being self-centered to being other-centered for the gospel. This kingdom offers a vision to live for, a vision large enough to encompass the transformation of the world.

Second, Mark's narrative leads readers to experience a fundamental change of perception—to see that this vision of the kingdom is large enough to live and die for, that is, to understand, in the face of all our human resistance, that God wants people to risk status, power, and even life to bring the liberating power of the kingdom to others. How does Jesus try to get the disciples to see and understand this? He teaches them, corrects their inappropriate behavior, tells them about his own death, and gives them models—children, slaves, servants—to show them what they are to be like. He explains to them what they are not to be—kings who dominate, the wealthy who refuse to relinquish wealth, and those who want to acquire the world.

But, in the end, Jesus' greatest witness to new sight is his own life. Can the disciples see this man as the Son of God, as the definitive agent of God's rule? He exercised the power of the kingdom on behalf of others to the point where he was rejected by society's leaders, abandoned by the crowds, betrayed by friends, not exercising his power over others, misunderstood by all, and dying as a result of opposing the oppressive authorities. If the disciples can see revealed in this man who was executed the embodiment of God's idea of true greatness (15:2, 18, 26), then they will have seen the world upside down. They will see that God wants people to bring life for others even when they end up being killed for it! Thus, at the crucifixion, God's full standards of judgment for humans are revealed. And the resurrection of Jesus is God's affirmation that the way Jesus lived and the courage with which he died in the service of the good news is the way for all humans to live.

Third, Mark's narrative empowers readers to follow Jesus. As presented by Mark, Jesus' courage is more than example and revelation. Jesus' commitment in the face of execution empowers people to live for the good news in the face of rejection and loss. The narrative empowers readers to do this by leading them to identify with Jesus. The narrative distances readers from identification with the Judean and the Gentile leaders, because these leaders will kill others to save themselves. The narrative initially leads readers to identify with the disciples. However, when the disciples betray or abandon Jesus to save themselves, readers distance themselves from the disciples. In the end, readers identify with Jesus, because he is the one heroic figure left in the story. Jesus is afraid and does not want to die, yet he is willing to do what God wills for him, namely, to remain faithful to the good news of the kingdom in spite of the cost (14:39). Readers identify with the courage of Jesus and come away from the story saying, "I too want to be courageous in the face of death." Mark leads readers not so much to believe something about Jesus as to be like Jesus.

The narrative also empowers by purging readers of fear. Through identification with Jesus, readers face the experience of abandonment, rejection, mocking, physical suffering, and death. By going through Jesus' death in the experience of the narrative, readers face vicariously the fears that might otherwise paralyze them. And when the Gospel ends abruptly and shockingly with the women running away from the empty grave, terrified and saying absolutely nothing to anyone ("for they were afraid," 16:8), it is the readers who are left to tell this story.[3] And the readers are led to say, "I will not be frightened into flight or silence as the disciples and the women were. I will face up to my past failures and go on. I will tell about this even if it means persecution and death." At the end of the narrative, when all the characters in the story have failed to proclaim the good news about Jesus, the readers themselves will complete the Gospel by proclaiming with courage. In Jesus' absence, they will live as Jesus lived, with faith and courage, until Jesus returns.

How can a life and a death effect such empowerment? I can best illustrate it with a story about a concentration camp for American prisoners in the Far East during World War II.

> In a concentration camp of American prisoners, the guards had so intimidated the prisoners and so violated every code of civilized treatment that conditions were horrible. The prisoners had tried to cope by a dog-eat-dog existence. To survive, each man was out for himself. Prisoners stole food and medical supplies for themselves, robbed from each other, ratted on other prisoners in order to get favors from the guards, and isolated new prisoners who came into the camp.
>
> One day as they were coming in from work detail and putting away the tools, it was discovered that a shovel was missing. The guards were irate and lined the prisoners up and threatened them.

Finally, the guards said, "If the person who stole that shovel does not come forward in ten seconds, we're going to shoot all of you."

After a long silence, one of the prisoners finally stepped forward, at which point the guards pounced on him, beat him with their gun butts, and then shot him to death.

When the guards told the prisoners to finish putting away the tools, a strange thing was discovered. All the shovels were there. No shovel had been missing after all. In shock and silence, the prisoners went back to their barracks.

It took a while for it to sink in that one of the prisoners had voluntarily given his life so that the rest would not be shot, and gradually the attitudes of the prisoners began to change in the camp. Other acts of sacrifice began to take place. Prisoners began to share medical supplies with each other and formed teams to attend to each other's wounds and illnesses. Some made artificial limbs for those who had lost a leg or an arm in the war. Some sick prisoners in the camp actually gave up their food to weak prisoners who had a greater chance for survival. Others risked death by sneaking outside the camp to procure extra food for the sick. They established a secret system of communication to give each other information and support. They welcomed new prisoners and quickly incorporated them into their network. The generosity was contagious.

In the midst of the most horrible conditions, there emerged a remarkably humane society of prisoners, all made possible because of the effect of this one fellow prisoner who gave his life for them to live.

And just as the example of the one man empowered the other prisoners, just so the telling of the story empowers us to transfer that empowerment to our lives.[4]

In a similar way, Mark portrays Jesus' death as liberating and empowering. In Mark's portrayal, Jesus does not die so that sins might be forgiven (Jesus freely offers forgiveness apart from his death—2:5); rather, his courage to live for others in the face of execution liberates others from the grip of self-preservation in order that they too might live for others, even in the face of loss or persecution. Jesus' whole life, death, and resurrection liberate people from the self-oriented fear of death and empower them to live courageously for others, thereby creating humane communities of mutual service. And even if the readers have themselves stumbled before in the face of persecution, they now see new hope from the story, for Jesus remained loyal to his own frightened and stumbling disciples. Even after the disciples failed the ultimate test of discipleship, Jesus promised to go ahead of the disciples—including Peter, who denied him—in order to begin the mission anew from Galilee (16:7). The narrative thus encourages readers to recommit themselves to proclaiming the good news, in spite of their fear and in spite of ongoing threats. The narrative leads readers to live out and bring in the kingdom *now*, even before it comes fully.

Markan Trajectories

Down through history, the standards of the Gospel of Mark have been reflected in people who have lived courageous lives of service for others. Markan Christians are represented in the orders of the church that called people to give up their livelihood and security to preach the gospel or care for the poor and the ill. Countless missionaries who have left home, possessions, and security to bring the gospel and to serve in other parts of the world belong in the Markan trajectory. In modern times, their numbers will include those who risked their lives to rescue Jews in Nazi Germany. Mother Teresa and all who are inspired to be like her are to be counted among Christians who live out Mark's vision. And we might point to all who joined the struggle for civil rights in the United States. In all nations where people have struggled in nonviolent ways to free themselves from oppression—in Latin America, in South Africa, in the former Soviet Union, and in Asia—people have turned to Mark for courage to take risks in the fight against injustice. Contemporary psychologist Ernest Becker has articulated well Markan-type portraits of destructive people who dominate out of a fear of death and of life-giving people who are empowered with courage to live for others.

Especially for Mark, the kingdom belongs to ordinary folks, unnamed and unrecognized, who have quietly served their families or neighbors or someone in need. These are people who in very common situations courageously stand up to injustice, who speak up when others are silent, or who advocate on behalf of others. These are people who have an active sense of God's daily work in the world and who seek to foster it in any way they can. They carry out their occupations as vocations of caring service. Perhaps because Mark was written from a peasant perspective and portrays Jesus as a marginalized figure, many groups of poor and oppressed people have turned to Mark for the empowerment that comes from knowing that they are not alone in their struggle. Many people who daily face discrimination and deprivation— such as Hispanic American and African American men and women—have turned to Mark, where they find Jesus to be a very human figure who is in radical solidarity with them and who struggles with them in their plight. Also, many communities of women have found encouragement from Mark's challenge for men to relinquish their power over women, from Mark's portrayal of faithful female followers, and from Mark's call for service in a "discipleship of equals."[5]

Example of a Markan Community

A hypothetical community shaped by Mark's vision of the gospel would have an outgoing mission rooted in the activity of God in the world. This might be a stripped-down version of Christian community with little structure, limited ritual, and a few basic affirmations, in order that the focus might be on commitment and action. Participants would see themselves as an alternative community unconcerned with the quest for power, wealth, and status. As an alternative to the values of the culture, the Markan community would seek to create an oasis of the kingdom now and would seek to spread the kingdom as leaven in the world. They would be active in their daily lives to serve the needs of others and to overcome oppression in the society. The community might be composed of people courageously struggling to overcome their own poverty and oppression, or they might be people risking status and power in solidarity with the marginalized. Or they may be people who use their positions of power as opportunities to serve those without power. They would make sacrifices and take risks in their radical commitment to the work of God. Because no one is to lord it over another in the community, leadership would be shared by all in service to one another. People would work out conflicts and differences as a whole community without disciplining or shunning. Their organization, their worship, their storytelling, and their giving would all be oriented toward building up the courage to be God's people and to bring God's kingdom to the world in the face of any obstacle.

Notes

1. Other scholars place Mark's Gospel in Rome after the Neronian persecution of the early sixties. Interpreting Mark in the context of this different social location will result in a different understanding of this Gospel.

2. The translation of Mark used in this chapter is the author's own. See chapter 1 of *Mark as Story: An Introduction to the Narrative of a Gospel* (Philadelphia: Fortress Press, 1982).

3. Scholars now generally agree that the Gospel of Mark originally ended at 16:8, and that other endings extending the Gospel were added by later scribes.

4. This story is based on an incident recounted in an autobiographical work about a Japanese concentration camp in Thailand during World War II, *Through the Valley of the Kwai*, by Ernest Gordon (New York: Harper, 1962). The work is a remarkable story of people who discovered a humane way of living in consonance with the portrait of the kingdom of God in Mark.

5. The phrase is from Elisabeth Schüssler Fiorenza's book *In Memory of Her*. Mark is antipatriarchal. Disciples leave fathers, but they do not gain them in the new community (10:28–30).

Further Reading

Achtemeier, Paul. *Invitation to Mark: A Commentary of the Gospel of Mark with a Complete Text from the Jerusalem Bible*. Doubleday, 1978.

Anderson, Janice Capel and Stephen Moore, editors. *Mark and Method: New Approaches to Biblical Studies*. Minneapolis: Fortress Press, 1992.

Beck, Robert. *Non-Violent Story: Narrative Conflict Resolution in the Gospel of Mark*. Maryknoll: Orbis, 1996.

Becker, Ernest. *Denial of Death*. New York: Free Press, 1985.

_____. *Escape from Evil*. New York: Free Press, 1975.

Best, Ernest. *Mark: The Gospel as Story*. Edinburgh: T.&T. Clark, 1983.

Brock, Rita Nakashima. *Journeys by Heart: A Christology of Erotic Power*. New York: Crossroad, 1988.

Dewey, Joanna. "Mark," in *Searching the Scriptures: A Feminist Commentary*, volume 2, edited by Elisabeth Schüssler Fiorenza. New York: Crossroad, 1994, 470–510.

Elizondo, Virgil, editor. *Way of the Cross: The Passion of Christ in the Americas*. Maryknoll: Orbis, 1992.

Hurtado, Larry. *Mark*. The Good News Commentary Series. New York: Harper and Row, 1983.

Juel, Donald. *A Master of Surprise: Mark Interpreted*. Minneapolis: Fortress Press, 1994.

Keenan, John P. *The Gospel of Mark: A Mahayana Reading*. Maryknoll: Orbis, 1995.

Kelber, Werner. *Mark's Story of Jesus*. Philadelphia: Fortress Press, 1979.

Kinukawa, Hisako. *Women and Jesus in Mark: A Japanese Feminist Perspective*. Maryknoll: Orbis, 1994.

Myers, Ched. *Binding the Strong Man: A Political Reading of Mark's Story of Jesus*. Maryknoll: Orbis, 1988.

Nelson-Pallmeyer, Jack. *Brave New World Order: Must We Pledge Allegiance?* (especially chapter 8). Maryknoll: Orbis, 1992.

Nicolson, Ronald. *A Black Future? Jesus and Salvation in South Africa*. Philadelphia: Trinity Press International, 1990.

Pallares, Cárdenas José. *A Poor Man Called Jesus*. Maryknoll: Orbis, 1990.

Piers, Alysius. *An Asian Theology of Liberation*. Maryknoll: Orbis, 1988.

Rhoads, David and Michie, Donald. *Mark as Story: An Introduction to the Narrative of a Gospel*. Philadelphia: Fortress Press, 1982.

Schüssler Fiorenza, Elisabeth. *In Memory of Her: A Feminist Theological Reconstruction of Christian Origins*. New York: Crossroad, 1983.

Stock, Augustine. *Call to Discipleship: A Literary Study of Mark's Gospel*. Wilmington: Michael Glazier, 1982.

Sugirtharajah, R. S., editor. *Voices from the Margin: Interpreting the Bible in the Third World*. London: SPCK, 1991.

Tesfai, Yacob, editor. *The Scandal of a Crucified World: Perspectives on the Cross and Suffering*. Maryknoll: Orbis, 1994.

4
The Gospel of Matthew
Righteousness before the Law

Background and Purpose

THE GOSPEL OF MATTHEW WAS PROBABLY WRITTEN to a predominantly Judean Christian audience in an urban setting, perhaps Antioch of Syria. Because of its late date and its literary dependence on Mark, scholars generally agree that this Gospel was not written by the disciple of Jesus named Matthew. The anonymous writing was probably penned by a scribe or rabbi who believed that Jesus was the Messiah. For the sake of convenience, we will refer to the author as Matthew.

The Gospel of Matthew was probably written between 80 and 90 C.E., about ten to twenty years after the Roman-Judean War of 66 to 70 C.E. The two main groups in Israel to survive that war were liberal Pharisees and liberal Judean Christians, liberal in the sense that they had opposed the war and were open to relations with Gentiles. After the war, the Pharisees set up a school at Jamnia under the leadership of Rabbi Johanan ben Zakkai in order to reinterpret the Law of Israel in light of the destruction of Jerusalem and the Temple. These Pharisees wanted to establish their view of the Law as normative for Judeans everywhere.

The Judean Christians who survived the war also wanted influence over Judean beliefs and practices. Matthew's community was likely one such Judean-Christian synagogue. Like the Pharisees, these Judean Christians believed they had the correct interpretation of the Law of Israel. Matthew wrote to reinforce for his community that the Messiah had already come in the person of Jesus and had given the authoritative interpretation of the Law. Therefore, the Pharisees should not now interpret the Law otherwise.

Matthew also wanted to show that the Judean leaders could have avoided Israel's war with Rome. In Matthew's view, if the Judeans in Israel had listened to Jesus' teaching about the Law, they would have loved the enemy, refused to fight the Romans, and avoided the war. Jesus taught that "all who live by the sword will die by the sword" (26:52) and that "the gentle (meek) . . . will inherit the earth" (5:5). Matthew's story shows, on the one hand, how the Judeans in Israel who rejected Jesus' way for Israel came to "die by the sword" and, on the other hand, how the Judeans who accepted Jesus' way were now inheriting the earth by spreading the Gospel among the Gentile nations of the world.

Obviously, there are many themes and patterns in Matthew that are similar to Mark, especially so because Matthew used a great deal of material from Mark in the writing of his Gospel. I will focus on the distinctive pattern of the two contrasting ways that emerge primarily in Matthew's depiction of Jesus' teaching.

The Two Ways: The Law Interpreted by Pharisees or the Law Interpreted by Jesus

In Matthew, the contrasting ways of life represent a conflict between two different ways to interpret God's will, two contrasting ways to live out the Law of Israel (the Torah, the first five books of the Hebrew Bible or Old Testament). As portrayed in Matthew's narrative, the interpretation of the Law by the Judean leaders, particularly the Pharisees, leads to hypocrisy. For Matthew, hypocrisy is a double standard that makes behavior appearing outwardly to be good end up being destructive. In Matthew's view, the Pharisees have a right and a responsibility to interpret the Law on behalf of the people of Israel, but they do not go far enough in applying the Law (5:20); they do not assist people in carrying out the Law (23:4, 13–15); and their own behavior contradicts their teaching (23:2–3). As leaders, they do not set a good example, and they are destructive. The result is an unjust society of conflict and strife. Therefore, they are not to be followed. On the other hand, the interpretation of the Law by Jesus, in Matthew's portrayal, empowers people to carry out the full measure of the Law in righteous integrity and without hypocrisy, which brings life and salvation. The result of such behavior will be a just society. As leader of the people, Jesus the Messiah lives what he teaches and is therefore a model to follow. Like Mark, Matthew uses characterization to show the two ways. Matthew also expresses the two ways in Jesus' extensive ethical teaching and in the parables.

Here are the characteristics of the two ways:

The Law Interpreted by Pharisees	The Law Interpreted by Jesus
Leads to hypocrisy	Makes integrity possible
Limited application of Law	Full application of Law
Places Law on people as a burden	Jesus' yoke is light
Blindness, self-deception	(In)sight into self and God
Double-minded	Purity of heart
Destructive	Life-giving/gentle/meek
Neglect of the least	Care for the least
Judgmental woes	Empowering blessings
Evil	Righteousness
Injustice in the nation	Society with justice
National destruction	Inherit the earth
Will weep and gnash teeth	Will shine like the sun

The plot of Matthew's Gospel follows the fate of the two main character groups: the leaders of Israel who reject Jesus, and the disciples who follow him. On the one hand, the leaders in Israel who come to reject Jesus are foreshadowed in the birth narratives by Herod, who pretends to worship the King Jesus but who really wants to murder him (2:8). As the story progresses, the Judean authorities likewise oppose Jesus and seek to trap him. In the Woes (23:1–39), Jesus condemns the Pharisees and their scribal experts in the Law for their hypocritical destructiveness (23:1–39). At the end of the story, the leaders coalesce their opposition to Jesus when they stir up the crowd to call for Jesus' death, "Let his blood be upon us and upon our children" (27:25). Matthew portrays this declaration as a prophecy of the fate of this group, for he considers that their rejection of Jesus and of his teaching led to their destruction in the Roman-Judean War (23:37–39). At the final judgment, those who have chosen the path of destruction will be "weeping and gnashing their teeth" (25:30, 46).

On the other hand, the Judean (and Gentile) followers who eventually come to embrace Jesus' way are foreshadowed in the birth narratives by the wise men, who come from afar sincerely seeking to worship Jesus (2:1–12) and by the righteous Joseph, who shows integrity in his response to Mary's pregnancy (1:19). Later, the adult Jesus blesses a new community into being (5:1–12). Then, in the Sermon on the Mount, Jesus presents the interpretation of the Law that should characterize this community and result in righteousness without hypocrisy (5:13–7:27). Many Judeans respond favorably to Jesus' teaching and to his healing, and Jesus calls twelve disciples. About halfway through the story, Jesus gives authority to his disciples and establishes this new community as the church (16:17–19). However, at the time of Jesus' death, the disciples stumble. Nevertheless, in a resurrection appearance, Jesus reaffirms the leadership of the disciples, and he now commissions his followers to go to all the diverse Gentile nations of the earth baptizing people and teaching them to obey Jesus' commandments (28:16–20). At the final judgment, the disciples will sit on thrones judging the twelve tribes of Israel (19:28), and all who have chosen the way of Jesus will "shine like the sun in the realm of their Father" (13:43).

The narrative guides the readers to reject the way of the Pharisees and to accept the way of Jesus. As readers listen to the teaching of Jesus, they see the hypocrisy of Israel's leaders through Jesus' eyes and at the same time they learn what it means to follow Jesus. The account of Jesus' execution reinforces the readers' rejection of the Judean leaders. In turn, the account of the resurrection secures the readers' commitment to the mission of the new community.

Before we consider fully Matthew's perspective, a reminder about the danger of anti-Judaism is in order. Because Matthew's community was in conflict with Pharisees in *his time*, his story about *Jesus' time* in the past manifests an especially virulent attitude against the Pharisees. Matthew portrays the Pharisees as a brood of vipers, as white-washed tombs, and as legalistic, hypocritical, and self-righteous leaders. Indeed, in our time, because of such a portrayal, the very word *Pharisee* has come to denote a hard-hearted hypocrite. Matthew's own polemic actually extends beyond the Pharisees to include all the Judean leaders and even the populace. For example, it is Matthew who deflects responsibility for Jesus' death away from the Romans, exonerates the Roman procurator for Jesus' death by having Pilate wash his hands of the matter (27:24), and blames Israel by having the whole crowd say, "His blood be on us and on our children" (27:25). In Matthew's view, the Roman-Judean War was the result of Israel's rejection of Jesus' way for the nation and for their execution of him.[1]

However, Matthew is not rejecting Judaism as such. Matthew claims that his Judean Christian movement is the true Judaism. Here are two siblings, Christian Judeans and Pharisaic Judeans, making exclusive claims for the heritage of Israel. Hence, Matthew is not repudiating Judaism but the Pharisaic interpretations and practices of Judaism as he portrays them.[2] Indeed, Matthew is the most Jewish of the Gospels: the Law remains valid, the Sabbath is preserved, dietary laws are not nullified, and the whole ministry of Jesus is a fulfillment of Law and prophets. In that time, believing in Jesus as the Messiah did not make one a non-Judean. However, as the smaller of the two groups that survived the war with Rome, Matthew's community defined itself in relation to the Pharisees with whom it had the most in common and with whom it was in conflict. As such, Matthew vilifies the Pharisees as a way to secure the identity of his own group.

We readers can counter anti-Judaism by seeing the conflict in Matthew in its historical context, by refusing to accept Matthew's stereotypes as accurate portrayals of real people, and by not projecting the conflict in the Gospel onto the present relationship between Jews and Christians. We can view Matthew's stereotypical portrayals of Pharisees and of Jesus' disciples as options for all readers to reject or to emulate. Thus, we may see the rhetoric of the narrative leading readers to choose not between Judaism and Christianity but between hypocrisy and righteous integrity.

As we have indicated, the behavior associated with each of the two ways is embedded in the whole narrative, but the contrasts are most clearly set out in the Sermon on the Mount (5:1–7:27) and in the Woes (23:1–39). In these two sections of the Gospel, Matthew lays bare the dimensions of destructive hypocrisy and life-giving integrity. What follows is based primarily on Jesus' teaching in these two sections of Matthew's Gospel.[3]

The Human Condition: Blind Hypocrisy

In Matthew, life lived under the Law as the Pharisees interpret it leads to blind hypocrisy. It is "blind" hypocrisy, because Matthew deals mainly not with the crass hypocrisy of people like Herod (2:8), who knowingly say one thing and intend to do another, but with people like the Pharisees who, in Matthew's portrayal, are attempting to be righteous and to do God's will yet who misunderstand God's will and are unaware of the inconsistencies in their misguided efforts. Matthew's problem is how to show readers that some people who appear to be good are really evil. Matthew deals with that conundrum by trying to expose for his readers the nature of blind hypocrisy. In Matthew's portrayal, hypocrites tell people to follow God's will, but they themselves do not follow it (23:3). Their evil comes from the fact that they apply the Law only to outward actions and to limited situations, which leads to hypocritical inconsistency.

In Matthew, the word *hypocrisy* refers to deceptive appearances due to a doublemindedness by which people are not consistent in their lives. The result is an incongruity reflected in such imagery as a lamp under a basket (5:15), salt that no longer preserves (5:13), sheep who are inwardly wolves (7:15), lights that are dark (6:23), a house built on sand (7:26–27), and guides who are blind (23:24). It is this inconsistency, this double-mindedness, this hypocrisy, this lack of integrity in human action that Matthew sees as the problematic human condition. And "unless your righteousness goes beyond that of the scribes and Pharisees, you will not enter the kingdom of God" (5:20).

There are four types of hypocrisy in Matthew. In one category are people whose inner motives contradict their outward actions. For example, people appear to do acts of righteousness to glorify God—alms, prayer, and fasting. However, they are really doing such acts to be glorified by others (6:1–18). Jesus warns them that if they do this they will indeed receive their reward in full (6:2); that is, they will be glorified by others, but they will get "no reward from your Father in heaven" (6:1). The hypocrites announce their charity in the markets (6:2) or pray in public (6:5) or "disfigure" their faces with ashes when fasting, all in order to impress people (6:16). In so doing, they store up treasures (of status) on earth (6:19), but they will get no reward from God (6:1), for they did not act in order to glorify God (5:16). In each case, the motive for the action—to be seen and honored by people—undermines the integrity of actions that outwardly appear to be in obedience to God's will. The approval from others serves to render such "religious" people blind and to lead them to think mistakenly that they really are righteous.

A second type of hypocrisy is similar to the first. Here, the inner attitudes are contrary to the outward appearances of righteousness. For example, people may never have murdered anyone, but they are full of anger. "You have heard that it was told the ancients, 'Do not murder' and 'Whoever murders will be liable to judgment.' But I tell you, whoever is angry with a brother or sister will be liable to judgment" (5:21–22). People may never have committed adultery, but they are full of lust (5:27–30). Such people are like cups that are clean on the outside but inwardly full of greed and self-indulgence (23:25). They are like white-washed graves, on the outside signaling cleanness, but on the inside full of dead peoples' bones—outwardly appearing righteous, but inwardly full of hypocrisy and wickedness (23:27–28). Again, the outward appearance of righteousness makes people blind to the double standard in regard to their inner disposition.

A third type of hypocrisy results when people act morally in some situations but not in others. For example, Jesus tells people "not to take an oath at all" (5:33–37). The implication of Jesus' prohibition of oaths is that if people take an oath their word will be good only when they are taking the oath, but their word might or might not be good when they are not taking an oath. Instead, Jesus says, "Let your word be 'Yes, Yes' or 'No, No' "—that is, *always* mean what you say. In this category belong also people whose love is limited, who love their neighbors but hate their enemies (5:43–48) or who love only those who love them in return. Jesus observes wryly that such people have done nothing special and deserve no reward, because even the tax collectors and Gentiles "do the same." Also, Israel's leaders honor the prophets of old by building memorials to them, but they blindly persecute the prophets that God sends to them in the present (23:29–31). Pharisees stringently tithe their house spices of mint and dill and cumin but neglect the more important parts of the Law—justice, mercy, and faithfulness. As Jesus says, "You strain a gnat out (of your food), then proceed to gulp down a camel" (23:23–24). In this type of hypocrisy, the Pharisees think that their strict adherence to many requirements fulfills the observance of the whole Law, while they are neglecting the major demands of the Law.

A final category of hypocrisy involves the inconsistency of relating to God one way and treating others another way, such as loving God and not loving the neighbor (22:34–40); bringing a gift for God without first being reconciled to others (5:23–24); asking God for what you want but not doing for others what they want (7:7–12); assuming God will forgive you when you do not forgive others (6:14–15); or expecting you will not be judged when you judge others (7:1–5). Such people address God's son as "Lord," yet they do not do the will of their Father in heaven (7:21–23). Other examples in Matthew include presuming to serve God while storing up treasures on earth (6:19–20) or having faith in God but worrying over food and clothing (6:25–34). These people honor God with the lips, but their hearts are far from God (15:8). In this category of hypocrisy, blindness comes from thinking we can separate our relationship with God from our relationships with other people.

In all these expressions of hypocrisy, there is something wrong on the inside, in the hearts of people. The interior motivation, the inner disposition, and the limited commitment to goodness are signs that the inside is warped and flawed. The whole person must be changed before righteousness can occur, for one does not harvest grapes from thorn bushes or figs from thistles (7:16), and a bad tree brings forth rotten fruit (7:17–18). Something is wrong with the hearts of people who do not produce good fruit; they are not pure of heart. And if something is wrong on the inside, even fruit that appears to be good is bad.

Matthew's story leads readers not to condemn others but to examine themselves for hypocrisy, not to point fingers at the hypocrisy of others but to discern their own hypocrisy, not first to take the sliver from the eye of another but to notice first the board in their own eye (7:3–5). Failure to remove this board is the willful blindness at the heart of hypocrisy. And when we combine blind hypocrisy with missionary zeal, we have the worst situation—blind guides who "shut the door to the kingdom of God in people's faces and do not enter themselves" (23:13), who go to great lengths to convert others and end up making them "twice the children of hell they are" (23:15), who "lay heavy burdens on people's shoulders and do not raise a finger to lift them" (23:4). This is religion at its most destructive, a manner of living that misleads people and destroys the very fabric of a society.

In any age it is difficult to talk about hypocrisy, because it is so easy for us to see the hypocrisy of others and so difficult for us to see hypocrisy in ourselves. We humans are very adept at self-deception. Even when we want to see our hypocrisy, it is not easy to discern. It takes a genuine commitment and a willingness to listen to hard words about ourselves from others. When we are part of a community that has oppressed others, it is difficult to see and to rectify what we have done. When we are a community that has historically been oppressed, we can see clearly the hypocrisy in the oppressors but are often blind to the oppressions between groups in our own community. And religion often becomes an insidious means to mask our hypocrisy, because we use the claim to sacredness as a shield against self-examination and criticism. True repentance involves a repudiation of hypocrisy, a willingness to ferret out self-deception, and a commitment to bear moral fruit that demonstrates the authenticity of repentance.

In our time, members of Alcoholics Anonymous may provide a good example of one way to deal with hypocrisy, for members of A.A. know the games people play in the syndrome of self-denial. We could all benefit from the ruthless honesty about ourselves that is required for such a program to work. We Christians would do well to settle in for an ongoing process of self-discovery, and we would do well at various points in our lives to share with another person a "fearless moral inventory" of ourselves. A Christian community could provide the safety and support necessary to enable us to look at ourselves—not only as individuals, but also as a church, as an ethnic group, as a nation, and so on. Asking and offering forgiveness, seeking reconciliation, and finding ways to rectify wrongs may be natural consequences of the process of facing squarely our hypocrisy.

In all of this, we need to be careful not to limit a commitment to integrity within the realm of individual moral behavior. When we use the English word *righteousness*, we may often mean individual goodness in matters of private morality. Yet, in Greek, the word *righteousness* is the very same word as *justice.* Try translating Matthew in such a way that every time you come across the word *righteousness* you substitute the word *justice.* Like the Old Testament prophets, Matthew is calling for the kind of personal righteousness that brings justice to the nation. For Matthew, the church is the household of God where such relationships of justice are modeled for the world. However, this commitment to justice is not limited to the church, because the "hungering and thirsting for justice" is meant to overcome discrimination in the public realm and enable the kingdom of God to take shape in the common life.

The Vision for Human Life: Righteous Integrity

The vision for human life is that people be like God, because God has integrity of purpose, speech, and action. Matthew states the goal in this stark way: "Be perfect . . . as your heavenly Father is perfect" (5:48). This statement follows the discussion about loving your enemy. If we want to be children of our heavenly parent, if we would be like God, we will love our enemies as well as our friends because God provides sunshine and rain for both the wicked and the good (5:45). To be perfect is to be mature and consistent in love—to love with a pure heart and to do it for all people, not just those who benefit you in return. To be perfect is to interpret the Law and to live the Law entirely through the prism of love for God and for the neighbor.

To be perfect, therefore, is to be single-minded in the pursuit of righteousness, "true" as one is true to a lover or true to a cause, with integrity of thought, speech, and action. For Matthew, being "perfect" is not a matter of engaging in a legalistic adherence to the letter of the Law. Rather, it is devotion to the will of God, to God's full intention or goal for mature human beings in community—righteous justice with mercy (9:13; 12:7). It is commitment from the heart that goes deeper than external fulfillment and broader than the overt extent of the Law. As such, perfection is fulfillment of the Law as Jesus interprets it and lives it. This is the "righteousness" that God calls forth from people.

To be perfect like God means to have integrity. People with integrity let their light shine in order that others may glorify God (5:16). To avoid glorifying themselves, they will do righteousness without fanfare, give charity so that the left hand does not know what the right hand is doing, pray in private, and fast without display (6:1–18). Having integrity means that an outward avoidance of murder and adultery reflects a heart that does not indulge in anger and lust (5:21–30). It means that people are always as good as their word (5:33–37), that they love others without regard for how others treat them (5:43–48), and that they attend not just to the minutiae of the Law but to justice, mercy, and faithfulness (23:23). Finally, it means that people will treat others as they want God (and others) to treat them (7:12)—showing mercy, not judging, providing for their needs, seeking reconciliation. Such goodness comes from people whose hearts, words, and actions are in harmony. People who act with such integrity are like the good tree that brings forth good fruit (7:17), the house built on rock (7:24–25), the preserving salt of the earth (5:13), and the light for the world (5:14). Such integrity provides the bonds that hold a just society together.

Matthew depicts Jesus as the one who manifests that kind of integrity. In Matthew, Jesus obeys every word that comes from the mouth of God (4:4), and his life is a fulfillment of God's will. Jesus displays an integrity in relation to God's will as depicted in the Blessings (5:1–12):

Blessed are the humble in spirit. . . .

Blessed are those who grieve (over the ills of the world). . . .

Blessed are the gentle. . . .

Blessed are those who hunger and thirst for righteousness. . . .

Blessed are the merciful. . . .

Blessed are the pure in heart. . . .

Blessed are the peacemakers. . . .

Blessed are those who endure persecution in the pursuit of righteousness. . . .

These traits represent the true spirit by which the Law is to be carried out. Such perfection, such integrity, may best be expressed by people who are unaware of "being righteous." In Matthew's depiction of the righteous at the last judgment, those who clothe the naked and visit the prisoners and feed the hungry do so without even being aware that they were doing it for Christ or that they would be rewarded for it (25:31–46).

In Matthew, Jesus lives out these traits in his life. In relation to ordinary folk whom he shepherds as the Messiah of Israel, he manifests gentleness, humility, and peacemaking. But Jesus is not so gentle with the other leaders of Israel, those whom he castigates for failure of leadership. Matthew himself may simply be inconsistent in his portrayal of Jesus. He may be betraying the dangers of legalism in his own form of religious expression. Or Matthew may be granting Jesus the exceptional right to condemn, because he is the one designated to judge at the endtime. Or it may be that Jesus treats ordinary folk, the lost sheep of the house of Israel, in a way different from the leaders of Israel who are neglecting and oppressing them. Part of the commitment to the lost sheep is to condemn those who are failing to provide them leadership. In any case, Jesus' harshness with the leaders is a caution not to assume that turning the other cheek means God will not hold accountable those who mistreat others.

Matthew clearly has high expectations of people. Contemporary readers of Matthew often experience the ethical teaching in Matthew as an impossible demand that we are not really expected to attain. On the contrary, Matthew simply has a very high view of what it means to be human and seems to assume that people can attain it in response to the power now available through Jesus. Matthew calls people to strive for *human excellence*. In our own time, we know what it means to strive for excellence in sports and business and the arts. Why should we be surprised if Matthew offers us a vision of what it means to be excellent as human beings? To be excellent in terms of moral integrity? To be excellent in terms of our relationships with others? After all, why should God not call forth from us everything we were created to be as human beings? In Matthew's view, Jesus has lived such a life, and we are called to learn from him and to follow. Matthew has a vision of a human community marked by righteousness, and he believes God is bringing that community into being for the world through the arrival of the kingdom.

The Transformation: A Relationship with Jesus of Blessing and Forgiveness

How do people create a just society? How do people escape the blind condition of hypocrisy in order to achieve the integrity necessary for righteousness? How do people change so that they are able to bring forth good fruit? How do nations come to feed the hungry and clothe the naked?

In Matthew, the key to this transformation is that people come into a discipling relationship with Jesus. This discipling relationship with Jesus is initially possible because people repent. Real repentance can change the heart; it is a turning away from sinful behavior to embrace the possibilities offered by the kingdom. Both John the Baptist and Jesus call for people to repent. On the one hand, many respond favorably to John's preaching and to Jesus' preaching. On the other hand, the Pharisees do not repent at John's preaching and, even when they see the tax collectors and harlots entering the kingdom of God, the Pharisees still do not repent.

Yet repentance is only the beginning of being a disciple of Jesus. Following Jesus is also a matter of obeying the Law as Jesus teaches it. How, for Matthew, does that become possible? It becomes possible because people really carry out the Law in relationship with the Messiah who interprets and lives the Law. Jesus says:

Come to me all you who are tired and burdened
   and I will give you rest.
Take my yoke upon you and learn from me
   for I am gentle and humble in heart,
   and you will find rest for yourselves.
For my yoke is easy and my burden light.
(11:28–30)

The Jesus of Matthew does not abrogate the Law. He clearly says, "I came not to undo the law but to fulfill it" (5:17). Like the Pharisees in Matthew, he lays the yoke of the Law upon people. However, unlike the Pharisees in Matthew, Jesus does not lay the Law as a burden on people and then withdraw and condemn people for their failure to keep it. Rather, he establishes a relationship of empowerment and support that enables people to carry out the Law. Such an approach to Law stands in contrast to the Pharisees, who in their teaching of the Law "tie up heavy burdens on people and lay them on people's shoulders, but they themselves do not want to lift a finger to help them" (23:4). Whereas converts to the Pharisees become hypocritical "children of hell" (23:15), converts to Jesus are able to carry out the Law in love because they are in personal relation with the Messiah who loves as God loves. Thus, even though Jesus interprets the Law in a more thoroughgoing and strict way than the Pharisees, his yoke is light because he enables people to bear it.

There are several dimensions to this relationship with Jesus that make the yoke easy and bring rest. First, the words of Jesus bring empowerment, for the transition to integrity begins with blessing (5:1–12). We tend to think of blessings as kindly affirmations. However, the Bible portrays a blessing as a powerful word bearing the capacity to carry out what is spoken. The blessings in Matthew announce a vision of excellence in human righteousness. They announce God's criteria of judgment ahead of the time of judgment and grant the assurance that those who live this way will be rewarded. As blessings, they empower people to incarnate the possibilities of this vision in the present time. They bless a new community into existence, a community in which people are merciful, hunger for justice, create peace, are pure in heart. The blessings inaugurate a new life under the rule of God by conveying the power to carry out the Law in its true spirit. Just as Jesus' words of healing in the Gospel effect physical wholeness for those who have faith, so his words of blessing create moral wholeness for those who will receive them. Jesus the Messiah establishes a relationship of empowerment by pronouncing these blessings.

A second dimension to this relationship with Jesus comes when Jesus exposes our failure to fulfill this vision of righteousness. Following the Blessings, Jesus gives an exposition of the Law in the Sermon on the Mount. Here Jesus interprets the Law so as to warn followers of the potential for double-mindedness. By a variety of concrete examples, Jesus seeks to break through the blindness and self-deception of the hearer in order to illuminate the depths of human hypocrisy. Here Matthew has a positive view of Law as that which reveals and illuminates. A story about Mahatma Gandhi may show how Jesus exposes hypocrisy and grants a vision of excellence in human righteousness.

> Before Gandhi was active in India, he lived in South Africa, in a small village populated by people from India. He was a magistrate, the village father-figure to whom people brought a wide range of problems to be solved.
> In this village there was a widow trying hard to raise a teenage son. In the absence of a father's authority, the child would not eat any healthy foods but would consume only candy full of sugar.

The widow knew that if Gandhi, the local father-figure spoke to the boy he would listen. She brought him to Gandhi and asked, "Will you talk to my son and tell him to stop eating sugar?"

Gandhi was silent for a moment and then said, "Would you bring the boy back to me a week from now?"

A week later, the woman brought the boy before Gandhi and asked again, "Will you now please tell my son to stop eating sugar?"

But Gandhi replied, "I'm sorry. Would you please bring him back in another week?"

A week passed, and the woman, desperate by now, came and again asked Gandhi to talk with her son. This time Gandhi carried out the woman's request. He resolved the problem by talking with the boy and telling him that it was imperative to stop eating sugar.

When Gandhi was finished, the woman took Gandhi aside, thanked him, and then asked him, "When we first came to you, you asked us to come back in a week. Then, when we came back, you asked us to come back in another week. Why did you do that?"

Gandhi replied, "Because I had not realized how difficult it would be for me to give up sugar."[4]

When people hear this story, there is often a laughter of insight and self-revelation. The response is often, "Aha! Yes, I see." In a moment of surprise, we see Gandhi's integrity and we see the extent of our own hypocrisy. Gandhi would not tell anyone else, even a child, to do something that he himself was not prepared to do. By contrast, we all too readily advise others to do what we ourselves do not do.

In a similar way to this story, the Sermon on the Mount exposes to us our hypocrisy by a series of insightful examples—how we pray to be seen by others, or how we live free of adultery but full of lust, or how we love only those who love us. In so doing, the sermon illuminates the depths of our human brokenness and lack of integrity. The Sermon on the Mount is so great because it cuts through the rationalizations, the self-imposed blindnesses, the games we play to reassure ourselves that we are "good" people, and it exposes the human condition for what it really is. At the same time, the Sermon grants new possibilities—of loving someone who does not love you, or of giving a shirt to someone who sues for your cloak, or of confessing your own faults rather than those of others. The whole Sermon engenders a series of "Aha! I see!" experiences. Thus, in the hands of Jesus the Messiah, the

Law is delightful because it grants wisdom, the gift of sight, the relief of finding out what is wrong with us, and the joy of discerning what we might become. The transition from hypocrisy to integrity involves an openness to the teaching of Jesus, a willingness to look at ourselves, and an eagerness to be exposed and empowered by his words. These features represent Matthew's understanding of the process of discipleship, a process that takes time and involves a community.

There is even more to this personal relationship with Jesus that empowers disciples. Jesus not only lifts a finger to help people bear the yoke of the Law; he lives and dies so that people might be enabled to carry out the Law. God tells Joseph to give to the baby the name "Jesus," because he will (by his life and death) "save his people from their sins" (1:21). At the last supper, Jesus says that his blood will be poured out for many "for the forgiveness of sins" (26:28). Matthew knows people will fail, but instead of lowering the standards, he offers new beginnings. The offer of forgiveness lightens the yoke of the Law. There is always the opportunity to be freed from past failures for fresh starts. And as we know from the parable of the king who forgave the great debt, the act of forgiveness is meant to empower people to forgive others (18:21–35). With such experiences of liberation from sins, disciples become eager to confess the sins that burden them and to forgive the sins that burden others—"seventy times seven" (18:22).

The relationship with Jesus also offers spiritual nurture. Through Jesus' death and resurrection, Jesus continues to be available to followers (28:20). In the birth narratives, Jesus is named "Emmanuel" (1:23), meaning "God is with us." In his teaching, Jesus says that where two or three are gathered in his name, "There I am, in their midst" (18:20). And the risen Jesus assures the disciples that he will be "with you all your days, until the end of the age" (28:20). Thus, the risen Jesus is available as a spiritual presence, granting confirmation and affirmation.

Finally, Jesus establishes a relationship not just with himself but also with God as Father: "All things have been committed to me by my Father . . . and no one knows the Father except the Son and those to whom the Son chooses to reveal the Father" (11:27). Israel had always known God as Father. However, the dominant images for God were those of remote figures, such as a king or a lord. By contrast, in Matthew, the depiction of God as Father is paramount. In Matthew's portrayal, the model of God as Father brings God near, into the orbit of familial relationships, establishing intimacy and care. As a means to experience the original freshness and power of the Father language in Matthew, read the Sermon on the Mount with all female imagery for God, for example, by substituting "Mother" where "Father" occurs. As a heavenly parent, our Mother in heaven knows what we need before we ask, provides food and clothing, teaches, reveals, commands, rewards, punishes, and forgives. This secure relationship with a heavenly parent provides the context whereby people can dare to imitate God, attain righteousness and integrity, and thereby glorify God by becoming "children of the Father" (5:45). In response to a relationship of secure love and forgiveness, God empowers people to be righteous. For Matthew, this is the glory of being human.

In summary, Matthew preserves the Law as Jesus interprets it and intends for people to fulfill it. Matthew shows that in the wrong hands Law can lead to self-deception, blindness, and destructiveness. However, in relation to Jesus, Law can overcome self-deception, bring insight, and generate a vision of integrity. Matthew has a "theology of character," for he seeks by his story of Jesus to create people who do righteous deeds of integrity in relation to a loving God, summarized in the commands to "love God" and to "love your neighbor as yourself." Such righteous behavior enables followers of Jesus to create a community that is a beacon of light in a dark world, that is leaven for a better society, providing the preserving salt that enables nations to thrive with mercy. At the final judgment, the determinative question (to the nations!) is: Did you feed the hungry, visit those in prison, clothe the naked, love the neighbor? (25:35–36). Jesus does not abolish Law; rather, he helps people to understand God's will and to fulfill it. In Matthew, God's activity in Jesus is the grace and power that enable people to strive—through the presence and forgiveness of Jesus—to fulfill the Law.

Matthean Trajectories

The trajectories of Matthew have led to the great traditions of ethical reflection, such as the work of Thomas Aquinas and the authority of canon law. In the modern period, the Anabaptist traditions, such as the Quaker and the Mennonite communities, have drawn upon the Sermon on the Mount as a major source of ethical reflection, especially related to issues of peacemaking. Discipleship traditions have seen in Matthew a model for learning from Jesus, following him, and going out to preach and baptize. The trajectory has continued in contemporary Christian reflection on social and personal issues such as disarmament, abortion, capital punishment, the environment, sexual morality, and business ethics. Papal encyclicals and denominational statements on ethical issues generally stand in this tradition of ethical reflection.

Many contemporary nonviolent movements of civil disobedience in the pursuit of justice, such as the civil rights movement of the sixties, have been guided by Jesus' principles of love for enemy and nonretaliation. Leaders like Mahatma Gandhi and Martin Luther King were directly influenced by the teachings in the Sermon on the Mount. Matthew's vision for justice has been the source of inspiration for many people committed to transform society. Advocates for the poor point to the parable of the last judgment for the Christian mandate to feed the hungry and clothe the naked. The Matthean trajectories are evident in the lives of individuals who in relationship to Jesus have struggled for personal integrity and righteousness.

Example of a Matthean Community

A contemporary Matthean group might be a community of people engaged in a process of being "discipled" by Jesus in the service of the kingdom of God. Members might cluster into small covenant groups and exercise a spiritual discipline, designed to get the support they need to make their words match their deeds. Leaders would be people of wisdom in the community, sages who could help people chart the Christian life.

Such a modern community based on Matthew's vision of the gospel would have morality at the center of life and action. This would be a community that was a place for moral discourse. It would have a deep sense of the goodness of God as a force for integrity in the midst of concrete daily living. Participants would focus their worship, education, and mission on expressing righteousness in the world. The community would seek justice not only, or even primarily, for themselves but for others, especially those whom they themselves may have wronged. In a process of truth-telling, they would be eager to discern all forms of hypocrisy in their lives and in the society. The community would make a covenant together to ferret out injustice and discrimination among themselves and in society. Members would engage regularly in self-examination and confession—at an individual and at a communal level. Worship would provide litanies of repentance for personal, ecclesial, national, and world sins, offer powerful declarations of forgiveness, and invite people to make covenants to act on behalf of a better world. Members would have a sense of God's guidance and the presence of Jesus as they struggled to deal with moral issues and worked for peace and justice in society.

This community would have a sense of being a family of God. They would seek to deal with offenses among members according to a fair process with kindness and firmness and without self-righteousness. This community would strive to be preserving salt and a guiding light in the common struggle for a just world.

Notes

1. The Roman-Judean War was a very complex event involving many causes and motives, not least of which was the desire to overthrow the Roman yoke. See *Israel in Revolution 6 to 74 C.E.*, by the author.

2. For a sympathetic treatment of Pharisees around the time Matthew was written, see *A Life of Johanan ben Zakkai* by Jacob Neusner.

3. The translations in this chapter are my own.

4. I heard this oral tradition years ago from a professional storyteller.

Further Reading

Alport, Gordon. *The Nature of Prejudice*. Reading, Mass.: Addison-Wells Publishing, 1986.

Anderson, Janice Capel. *Matthew's Narrative Web: Over, and Over, and Over Again*. Sheffield: JSOT Press, 1994.

Barndt, Joseph. *Dismantling Racism: The Continuing Challenge to White America*. Minneapolis: Augsburg, 1991.

Betz, Hans Dieter. *Essays on the Sermon on the Mount*. Philadelphia: Fortress Press, 1985.

Carter, Warren. *Matthew: Storyteller, Interpreter, Evangelist*. Peabody, Mass.: Hendrickson, 1995.

Crosby, Michael. *The Spirituality of the Beatitudes: Matthew's Challenge for First World Christians*. Maryknoll: Orbis, 1984.

Davies, W. D. *The Setting of the Sermon on the Mount*. New York: Cambridge University Press, 1964.

Gandhi, M. K. *What Jesus Means to Me*. Ahmedabad: Navajivan Publishing House, 1959.

Garland, David. *Reading Matthew: A Literary and Theological Commentary on the First Gospel*. New York: Crossroad, 1983.

Hallie, Philip. *Lest Innocent Blood Be Shed*. New York: Harper, 1979.

King, M. L. *Strength to Love*. Philadelphia: Fortress Press, 1981; original, 1963.

Kingsbury, J. D. *Matthew as Story*. 2d edition. Philadelphia: Fortress Press, 1986.

Knippel, Charles. *The 12 Steps: The Church's Challenge and Opportunity*. St. Louis: Concordia, 1994.

Levine, Amy-Jill. *The Social and Ethnic Dimensions of Matthean Salvation History*. Lewiston, N.Y.: Edwin Mellen, 1988.

Luz, Ulrich. *Matthew One to Seven: A Continental Commentary*. Translated by Wilhelm Linss. Minneapolis: Augsburg, 1992.

Malina, Bruce. *The New Testament World: Insights from Cultural Anthropology*, revised edition. Louisville: Westminster/ John Knox, 1993.

Malina, Bruce and Richard Rohrbaugh. *Social-Science Commentary on the Synoptic Gospels*. Minneapolis: Fortress Press, 1992.

Miller, Keith. *A Hunger for Healing: The Twelve Steps as a Classic Model for Christian Spiritual Growth*. San Francisco: Harper, 1991.

Neusner, Jacob. *A Life of Johanan ben Zakkai*, 2d edition. Leiden: Brill, 1970.

_____. *The Way of the Torah*. 5th edition. Belmont, Calif.: Wadsworth, 1993.

Overman, Andrew. *Matthew's Gospel and Formative Judaism: The Social World of the Matthean Community*. Minneapolis: Fortress Press, 1990.

Powell, Mark. *God with Us: Toward a Pastoral Theology of Matthew*. Minneapolis: Fortress Press, 1995.

Rasmussen, Larry. *Moral Fragments and Moral Community: A Proposal for the Church in Society*. Minneapolis: Fortress Press, 1993.

Rhoads, David. *Israel in Revolution 6 to 74 C.E.: A Political History based on the Writings of Josephus*. Philadelphia: Fortress Press, 1976.

Saldarini, Anthony. *Matthew's Christian-Jewish Community*. Chicago: University of Chicago Press, 1994.

Senior, Donald. *What Are They Saying about Matthew?* 2d edition. Mahwah, N.J.: Paulist Press, 1996.

Smith, Robert. *Matthew*. Minneapolis: Augsburg, 1989.

Stanton, Graham. *A Gospel for a New People: Studies in Matthew*. Louisville: Westminster/John Knox, 1992.

Stendahl, Krister. *Meanings: The Bible as Document and as Guide*. Philadelphia: Fortress Press, 1984.

Stock, Augustine. *The Method and Message of Matthew*. Collegeville: Liturgical Press, 1994.

Via, Dan O. *Self-Deception and Wholeness in Paul and Matthew*. Philadelphia: Fortress Press, 1990.

Wainwright, Elaine. *Towards a Feminist Critical Reading of the Gospel according to Matthew*. Berlin: de Gruyter, 1991.

5
The Gospel of Luke
Society with Mercy

Background and Purpose

THE GOSPEL OF LUKE WAS PROBABLY WRITTEN between 80 and 90 C.E., possibly in an urban area of Asia Minor. The author likely wrote out of an upper class context with a radical commitment to social justice and to the poor. The author of this Gospel also wrote "The Acts of the Apostles," a portrayal of the history of the church after the death of Jesus. Tradition attributed this Gospel to a physician named Luke, who traveled with the apostle Paul (Colossians 4:14). However, there are serious doubts among scholars about the accuracy of this tradition. Again, for convenience, we will refer to the author as Luke.

In the first lines of his Gospel, Luke tells us that other accounts of Jesus' life had preceded his Gospel (1:1–4). These written sources probably included Mark's Gospel and a collection of sayings of Jesus, along with other sources now lost to us. Luke probably did not have a knowledge of Matthew's Gospel, which was written in another location about the same time as Luke's Gospel. In Luke's view, his written sources had in turn depended on those who were "eyewitnesses and servants of the word," that is, those who first passed on the traditions about Jesus by word of mouth. Luke tells us that he has carefully investigated the events of Jesus' life and that he is writing his own orderly account so that readers "may know the truth concerning the things about which you have been instructed." Out of these traditions, Luke has created a powerful story with many complex themes. As with the other Gospel writers, Luke has exercised authorial creativity in shaping his story of Jesus as a means to expressing the true meaning of the events he is describing.

Luke probably directed his Gospel to a broad Gentile and/or Gentile Christian audience, although his audience probably also included Judeans and Judean Christians. In particular, he addressed the Gospel to a person with the Greek name of Theophilus (probably a patron, 1:3), which means "Lover of God." Perhaps "Theophilus" symbolically represented "God-lovers" or "God-fearers," Gentiles who attached themselves to the Judean synagogues, who worshiped the God of Israel, and who may have heard about Jesus. In his Gospel, Luke appeals to a broad Gentile audience by writing in a form similar to Greco-Roman histories of the time (1:1–4) and by dating events in relation to the Roman emperors (2:1; 3:1–2). Also, he proclaimed a message that could apply to everyone—a call to repentance and forgiveness. By this universal call, Luke sought to embrace not only diverse ethnic groups but also the rich and the poor, the powerful and the powerless, the elites and the marginalized.

As with the treatment of the other Gospels, I emphasize the distinctive themes of Luke's Gospel. Luke's whole narrative expresses the mercy and compassion of God. Luke shows God's love for everyone by emphasizing God's special compassion for the poor, the sick, the oppressed, the outcasts, and the sinners. In Luke, Jesus is a prophetic Messiah who promises followers the power to do miraculous acts of mercy for the sick and the needy. To receive such power, followers give themselves over to the merciful God who cares for the poor and the oppressed. Just as God cared for the lowly in Israel through Jesus, so God will care for Gentiles. In Luke's view, because Israel's leaders failed to heed Jesus, their power and wealth were taken from them in the war with the Romans (21:20–24). Likewise, if Gentile nations fail to share their wealth or to use their power to help people, their fate will be like the fate of Israel (21:24). Luke hoped that readers would become followers who received power to express compassion and proclaim the good news to the ends of the earth.[1]

The Two Ways: Society with Mercy or Society without Mercy

Luke roots his depiction of the human condition in the corporate life of the nation of Israel. In the birth narratives, Zechariah, Mary, Simeon, Anna, and others express hopes for the salvation of

Israel. As a prophet, Jesus addresses Israel as a whole. He confronts the capital city of Israel and weeps over the fate of Jerusalem (19:41). After Jesus' death, the disciples ask the risen Jesus, "Is this the time when you will restore the kingdom to Israel?" (Acts 1:6). Although the leaders of Israel rejected Jesus and his disciples, God redeems Jesus' tragic death for the larger purposes of the kingdom, using conflict and rejection to begin Israel's restoration through the new community of disciples (Acts 3:19–26). From beginning to end, Luke's Gospel is dominated by a concern for Israel's fate as a nation.

The overall plot of the story is that God anointed Jesus to address a nation with gross social inequities: the rich and the poor, the powerful and the lowly, the elite and the outcasts, the healthy and the sick, the full and the hungry, the "righteous" and the "sinners." Out of compassion for those who suffer, God has sent Jesus to champion the poor, heal the sick, and accept the outcasts—that is, "to seek and to save the lost" (19:10). The poor and the lowly respond to Jesus' teaching, and they follow him. At the same time, Jesus challenges the wealthy and the powerful to care for the poor and the lowly. But the wealthy and the powerful overwhelmingly reject Jesus' challenge. As a result, God will take away their wealth and their power. While the Gospel deals with the inequities only within the nation of Israel, Luke's critique applies to any nation with inequities in wealth and abuses of power (21:24).

Therefore, the two ways for this Gospel are reflected in the corporate life of the nation as a whole. The immoral way for a nation is to have great inequities in the society—an unequal distribution of wealth, a lack of justice, power in the hands of a small group who benefit themselves, and a great gulf between the haves and the have-nots. By contrast, the right way for a nation is expressed in the vision of society under the rule of God inaugurated by Jesus. Here the poor are cared for, debts are remitted, prisoners are freed, the outcasts are welcomed, the helpless are restored, and the hungry are fed.

In Luke, when Jesus confronts the inequities of Israel, he invites people to participate in a society under the rule of God, a new social order that fosters peace. The activity of John the Baptist guides people into "the way of peace" (1:79). At Jesus' birth, the angels announced "peace among those whom God favors" (2:14). Jesus taught the actions that would lead to peace. But the leaders of Israel rejected Jesus' message, because they did not know "the things that make for peace" (19:42). Therefore, Jesus ends up bringing not peace but division—a division between those dedicated to peace and those not dedicated to peace (12:51–53). Jesus is a winnower, who separates the wheat from the chaff (3:17). The result of the winnowing is that God will save by reversing the inequities.

Reversal is the key to Luke's story of Jesus. Out of compassion for the poor and the lowly, God will elevate those on the bottom who are victims of oppression, and conversely God will bring down those on the top who oppress the poor or fail to do anything for them. The reversal proves to be a disastrous upheaval in the life of the nation of Israel. The reversal in the life of Israel is most clearly stated in Mary's song to Elizabeth. Here the prophecy about what God will do through Jesus is stated in the past tense, as if the results were as good as done. By sending Jesus,

God has brought down the powerful from their thrones
and lifted up the lonely.
God has filled the hungry with good things
and sent the rich away empty.

(1:52–53)

This statement represents Luke's understanding of the nature and activity of God. It is a revolutionary statement about political realities—so revolutionary that even today in some parts of Central America, in the midst of oppression, the government has prohibited the church from repeating Mary's song in services of worship! Reinforcing this theme in the birth narratives is the speech of Simeon, who depicts Jesus as one who will cause this "rise and fall of many in Israel" (2:34).

This same dynamic of reversal is found in the teaching of Jesus. For example, the blessings in Luke are about actual poverty and lack of status in society, not spiritual humility, as in Matthew. And following the blessings there appear woes upon the wealthy, the comfortable, and those with high social status:

Blessed are you who are poor,
for yours is the kingdom of God.
Blessed are you who are hungry now,
for you will be filled.
Blessed are you who weep now,
for you will laugh.

> Blessed are you when people hate you
>> and when they exclude you,
>> revile you and defame you
>>> on account of the Son of Humanity.
> Rejoice in that day and leap for joy,
>> for surely your reward is great in heaven.
> For that is what their ancestors did to the prophets.
>
> But woe to you who are rich,
>> for you have received your consolation.
> Woe to you who are full now,
>> for you will be hungry.
> Woe to you who are laughing now,
>> for you will mourn and weep.
> Woe to you when all speak well of you,
>> for that is what their ancestors did to the false prophets.
>>> (6:20–26)

In Luke, Jesus develops these social reversals in his actions and words. He straightens (raises) the woman bent over for eighteen years and shames (brings down) the synagogue ruler who objects to this healing (13:10–17). Those who choose places of honor at a banquet will be asked to go down lower, while those at the lower places will be elevated (14:8–10). The rich man goes down to Hades, and the poor beggar is carried up to Abraham's bosom (16:19–31). The arrogant Pharisee who elevates himself is not justified, but the penitent tax collector who humbles himself is justified (18:9–14). Twice Jesus states that "all who exalt themselves will be humbled, but all who humble themselves will be exalted" (18:14; 14:11).

In addition to these "vertical reversals" of lifting up and bringing down, Jesus also depicts reversals regarding who is in and who is out. Jesus warns the religious leaders that they will be surprised when Gentiles from the east and west will sit at table with Abraham, while they themselves are cast out (13:28–30). The wealthy people invited to the banquet end up being excluded for their rejection of the invitation, while the marginalized—the poor, the maimed, the blind, and the lame—are brought in (14:15–24). In addition, God hides the realities of the kingdom from learned people but reveals them to children (10:21). "Some are last (least important) who will be first (most important), and some are first who will be last" (13:30).

The overall plot is itself a vertical reversal. The lowly man Jesus who is born in a stable to people in the hill country, who is greeted by humble shepherds, who in his life seeks to raise the fortunes of the lowly in Israel, and who dies in rejection and humiliation, will be raised from the dead and ascend into heaven to become lord of all (24:50–53). With him, the twelve apostles—from the lower classes of Galilee—will sit on twelve thrones judging the tribes of Israel (22:30). Meanwhile, the present rulers of Israel who exalt themselves will be brought down because they have shed innocent blood in killing Jesus. Jerusalem will be trodden down until the time of the Gentile domination over them is fulfilled (21:20–24; 19:41–44). Here Luke is undoubtedly referring to Israel's disastrous defeat at the hands of Rome within a generation after the death of Jesus. Jesus and the lowly are exalted, while Jerusalem and the leaders of Israel are humbled.

Thus, for Luke's Gospel, the two ways are rooted in the life of a nation. On the one hand, the negative way is national life without mercy, marked by oppressive inequities. God will not tolerate such disparity in wealth and abuse of power; therefore, God will elevate the lowly and bring down the oppressors from their thrones. On the other hand, the positive way is national life with mercy under the rule of God, marked by compassion and sharing. This is the vision that Jesus seeks to inaugurate among all who respond favorably to his invitation to enter the rule of God. The behaviors associated with these two ways are summarized in the following chart:

Society without Mercy	*Society with Mercy*
Oppress	Show compassion
Exclude the "sinners"	Include those who are "lost"
Love and hoard wealth	Give to the poor
Neglect the poor and the ill	Care for the poor and the ill
Put human things before God	Put God first
Exalt self	Humble oneself
Be foolish/blind	Be wise
Seek honor from people	Seek honor from God
Have hardness of heart	Repent and be forgiven
Love what people love	Love God above all else
Justify their own ways	Justify God's compassionate ways
Seek own interests	Be empowered by the Spirit

Luke depicts a society in which a small ruling elite held almost all the wealth and power, while the vast majority of people were peasants eking out a bare existence on the land. There was no middle class, and the peasants and artisans bore the burden of taxes to Israel and to Rome. Below the peasants were the sick and disenfranchised people for whom the bottom had dropped out.

How do we identify with such a situation when, in many ways, our own society in the United States offers a stark contrast to the economic conditions of the society depicted in Luke's Gospel? Many of us who live in America today have benefited from a society that has welcomed the tired and the poor and the huddled masses to a land of opportunity and vast resources. Indeed, in the latter half of this century, the United States succeeded in developing a broad middle class with a wide distribution of wealth. In relation to all the world's population, the vast majority of people who live in the United States today are in the upper 5 percent of people in the world in terms of wealth.

However, even the United States bears the stamp of the kind of society Jesus confronted in ancient Israel as Luke depicts it. Not all who live in America have benefited from our nation's wealth. The nation was established over the bodies of native peoples and the backs and bodies of slave labor from Africa. There are large numbers of people in this country who provided cheap labor for the nation's economy and who never got near the American dream. Furthermore, the United States has thrived because of the huge resources and cheap labor extracted from many impoverished countries. In recent decades, as part of a world trend, there has been a growing gap between the wealthy and the poor within the United States. The size of the middle class has eroded significantly. There is now a permanent underclass of working poor people. The difference in income between management and labor has grown by leaps and bounds. The real income of working people is much less than it was several decades ago. In comparison with most other industrialized nations, we have a greater portion of our people who are without health care and a greater portion of our children who live in poverty. The percentage of wealth in the hands of a small number of the people has greatly increased, and a larger number of people are below the poverty line. These inequities in wealth correlate with racial and ethnic discrimination and with differences in political power and influence. These inequities are also complicated immensely by the large federal deficit, the erosion of the environment, the spread of drug use, an increase in crime, and the presence of social unrest.

Thus, while we in the United States have very different social and economic circumstances from those in ancient Palestine, we nevertheless confront the same kinds of inequities in power, status, and wealth—within the United States and in relation to impoverished countries—that drove Luke to write his story about the God of compassion and "the things that make for peace."

The Human Condition: Society without Mercy Is Oppression

In Luke, oppression occurs in Israel because the leaders have failed to love God above all else. They love money (16:14). They exalt themselves above tax collectors and sinners (7:39). They like people to speak well of them (6:26). At one point, Jesus says, "What is prized by human beings is an abomination in the sight of God" (16:15). People in Luke's story value money, security, family, power, position, and status, more than they value God. The importance of seeking God's kingdom first is not a theme unique to Luke. Yet Luke emphasizes how the failure to put God first will result in great social inequities: the wealthy hoard money and the poor go hungry; the powerful use their power arrogantly and the lowly are oppressed and excluded. Those who do not love God with their whole hearts also do not love their neighbors as themselves (10:25–28).

In Luke, the wealthy put money above God and therefore do not share with the poor. They are greedy and define their lives by the abundance of their possessions (12:15). Riches choke them, and their lives do not produce fruit (8:14). Tax collectors and soldiers exploit people (3:12–14). The rich are full, they laugh, they are well-spoken of (6:24–26). A wealthy man refuses to give scraps to the poor beggar (16:21). Another builds barns to secure his own future and to take his ease (12:13–21). The Pharisees love money and store up fortunes on earth (16:14). The wealthy give only out of their surplus (21:4). The scribes confiscate the houses of widows (20:47). The leaders of Israel have made the Temple a "den of robbers" (19:45–48). Jesus condemns such people for ill-gotten wealth. Jesus also condemns people simply for having wealth when there are people who are poor, who have no food or clothing (18:18–30; 3:10). Thus, the rich young ruler had not stolen anything or defrauded anyone, and yet Jesus tells him to sell all he has and give to the poor (13:22).

Second, Israel's leaders show an arrogant use of power because they want to justify themselves in the eyes of others (16:15; 18:14). They presume on their privileged status as children of Abraham without bearing the fruit that God wants of Israel's guardians (3:7–8). They exalt themselves above others: a Pharisee is grateful because he is not like the tax collector (18:11), while others refuse contact with sinners (5:30; 7:39). The people in Jesus' hometown are furious that he will heal in Capernaum but not in Nazareth (4:23–30). The leaders of Israel will destroy to gain the inheritance of Israel for themselves (20:1–19). The objects of Jesus' prophetic vituperation are often people who, precisely because of their piety, think they have a right to separate themselves from others. They use their religion as a wedge between themselves and those who need their help: a prostitute, a half-dead man by the roadside, a tax collector.

In Luke's story, the elites of Israel care only for themselves, take care only for each other. They love only those who love them, do good only to those who return the favor, lend only to those from whom they expect to be repaid (6:32–36), and invite to banquets only those who can invite them in return (14:12–14). They do not have God's compassion and therefore do not bear the fruit God requires of those who love God. Because of their arrogance, the leaders neglect and oppress the poor, the sick, and the outcasts. The result is a society with gross inequities in wealth and abuse of power.

By implication, we get insights into the Judean leaders in Luke from Jesus' condemnation of them. The wealthy and the powerful are foolish (12:20). They acquire treasures that will fail instead of the true treasures in heaven (12:33; 18:18–25; 16:1–9). They seek honor from others rather than from God (16:15; 10:29). Rather than justify themselves in the sight of others, they should justify God's ways (7:29, 35), magnify God (Luke 1:46). They do not realize that unless they repent, they will perish. Because they do not repent, they do not experience God's merciful forgiveness for themselves. Because they have been forgiven little, they love little (7:47). The leaders foolishly reject the purposes of God for themselves (7:30) and do not know the compassion that makes for peace (19:42). In the end, they reject God's messengers, persecute God's prophets (11:49), and kill Jesus and those who follow him.

As a result, "Jerusalem will be surrounded by armies"; and those in Judea "will fall by the sword and be taken away as captives among the nations; and Jerusalem will be trampled on by the Gentiles" (21:20–24). Here, Luke sees the Roman-Judean War of 66–70 C.E. as the consequence of the failure of Israel's leaders to know "the things that make for peace."

The Vision for Human Life: Society with Mercy

In Luke, the goal for the nation is to place the compassionate God above all else. As portrayed in Luke, Jesus is the primary example of one who loves God above all. At twelve, Jesus says that he must be about his father's business (2:49). In the temptations, Jesus rejects worldly wealth and power, and he vows to worship God and serve him alone (4:8). After his baptism, Jesus is driven by the Spirit of God (4:1), and he enters Galilee "filled with the power of the Spirit" (4:14). Before every major event—baptism (3:21), healing (5:16), choosing the twelve (6:12), the messianic confession of Peter (9:18), teaching on prayer (11:1), transfiguration (9:28–29), and at Gethsemane (22:41)—Jesus is in prayer to God. Even as he dies, he commits his spirit into his Father's hands (23:46).

Jesus expects the same uncompromising allegiance to God from those who would follow him: "Whoever comes to me and does not hate father and mother, wife and children, brothers and sisters, yes, and even life itself, you cannot be my disciple" (14:26). He tells the twelve that "unless you give up all you have you cannot be my disciples" (14:33). To one who wants to bury his father, Jesus says, "Let the dead bury their own dead, but as for you, go and proclaim the kingdom of God" (9:59–60). To one who wants to say farewell to his family, Jesus says, "No one who puts a hand to the plow and looks back is fit for the kingdom of God" (9:62). To the woman who blesses his mother for having given birth to him, Jesus says, "Blessed rather are those who hear the word of God and obey it" (11:27–28). That is, people are to get their honor from God alone and not do the things that are valued by people. People are to take up their cross daily (9:23) in order to remove any and every obstacle to absolute allegiance to God.

What difference would this priority make in an individual life or in the life of the nation? For Luke, the distinguishing mark of life together is mercy: "Be merciful, just as your Father is merciful" (6:36). To put God above all else is to seek to be compassionate like God. The mercy of God drives the plot of Luke's story from beginning to end. Mercy is the recurring theme of the hymns to God in the birth narratives. Mercy is found in God's commitment to fulfill the promise to Abraham (1:55,72), in the ordinance of the Law to love the neighbor as oneself (10:25–37), and in the prophets' call for justice (4:18–19; 16:29–31). In Luke, the entire establishment of God's rule arises out of God's compassion for the poor. God seeks out the lost (15:3–10) and rejoices over one sinner who repents (15:3–24). The poor beggar Lazarus is carried to Abraham's bosom because God's heart has gone out to him for his misfortune. In a rather astounding statement, Luke claims that this God is "kind to the ungrateful and the wicked" (6:35), for mercy is God's way of bringing about change. Even God's relation to the leaders of Israel is driven by compassion. God's act in sending Jesus is a merciful warning to the proud before it is too late. Thus, God allows the gardener to tend the tree one more year before it is cut down (13:6–9). In the end, God's judgment upon the rulers is itself an act of liberating mercy that frees the oppressed (1:46–55, 68–79).

Mercy is central to Jesus' mission, as expressed in the programmatic statement of his mission:

The Spirit of the Lord is upon me;
because God has anointed me to bring
    good news to the poor.
God has sent me to proclaim release to the captives,
    and recovery of sight to the blind,
    to let the oppressed go free,
to proclaim the year of the Lord's favor.

                                                (4:18–19)

Jesus' activity liberates people from the tyrannies of illness, demons, and sin. The role of Jesus is encapsulated in one line: "For the son of humanity came to seek out and to save the lost" (19:10). In story after story—the healing of the centurion's slave (7:1–10), the raising of a widow's only son (7:11–17), the forgiveness of a sinful woman (7:36–50), the Samaritan who aids a stricken traveler (10:25–37), the father who welcomes a prodigal son (15:11–32), the tax collector who is justified for seeking God's mercy (18:9–14)—Jesus' message is compassion for the oppressed. When John the Baptist asks from prison if Jesus is the one to come, Jesus replies, "Go and tell John what you have seen and heard: the blind receive their sight, the lame walk, the lepers are cleansed, the deaf hear, the dead are raised, the poor have the good news brought to them" (7:22).

What happens when the wealthy put their trust in God first? When the wealthy love God and seek God's kingdom first, they trust God to provide for them. When God assures people of treasure in heaven, they are able to relinquish the treasures on earth that will fail. They can sell their possessions and give to the poor (12:33; cf. 11:41). Those who have two coats give to one who has none, and those who have more food than they need share it (3:11). Tax collectors and soldiers do not exploit people (3:12–14). Jesus announces the year of Jubilee, that legal provision for Israel whereby wealth is redistributed in the nation (4:19) by the pardon of debts, the release of indentured slaves, and the restoration of property. Jesus tells people to give to all who beg (6:30), to lend without expecting in return (6:35), to pardon debts (7:41–43), and to invite to dinner even those who are so poor that they cannot return the invitation (6:27–36; 14:12–14). Like the poor widow, they will give out of their need rather than just out of their surplus (21:4). Zacchaeus promises to give half his wealth to the poor and with the rest restore fourfold to those from whom he has extorted money, and Jesus responds by saying, "Today salvation has come to this house" (19:1–10). Mercy means that wealth will be shared by every means possible—individual (almsgiving), legal (Jubilee regulations), and institutional (implied by Jesus' attack on the extortion in the Temple) (19:45–46).

When the powerful love God first, they are humble and use their power in mercy to serve others (22:24–27). They act to justify God's ways rather than their own. They welcome outcasts, use the laws to help people, open the Temple for Gentiles. The leaders are to have compassion on lepers, beggars, slaves, widows, the hungry, the poor, women, tax collectors, sinners. Such people are to be included rather than excluded, elevated rather than trodden down, treated as the special objects of God's love rather than neglected. Even when the downtrodden are ungrateful or selfish, still the resolution to their situation is to be forged out in compassion (6:35). This is the fruit God desires from the tenants of the vineyard of Israel (20:10). There is no place for hoarding, arrogance, or exclusion. There is to be gracious giving and loving and acceptance.

Luke envisions that loving the merciful God above all else will lead to an equitable sharing of wealth and a humanitarian use of power. When compassion pervades every dimension of national life, the result will be a society that eliminates oppression and that meets the social and economic needs of people. Under the rule of God, this is accomplished by showing a special concern to care for the poor, the helpless, and the outcasts. Mercy undergirds the things that make for peace. For Luke, there is no peace without justice, and there is no justice without compassion.

The Transformation: Human Repentance, Divine Forgiveness, and the Power of the Holy Spirit

How do people acquire the capacity for mercy? How do people reorient priorities and love God above all else? How does God go about creating a society of compassion? For Luke, it is precisely because of God's active mercy that people are able to love God in return and to have compassion for others. It is the activity of the gracious God that empowers people—the God whose pleasure it is to give the kingdom (12:32), to give the Holy Spirit (11:13), to bring salvation, to offer the remission of sins.

For Luke, the key means of human transformation are repentance and forgiveness. In Luke, forgiveness is not connected to the death of Jesus. Jesus does not die for the forgiveness of sins or as a ransom for others. Jesus' rejection and death are the consequence of his prophetic ministry against oppressors and on behalf of the oppressed. Repentance and forgiveness are major themes of Jesus' whole ministry apart from any connection with his death. Jesus came to call "sinners to repentance" (5:32). Israel's leaders had labeled the peasants who did not observe the Judean Law as the "sinners." Ironically, however, the real sinners turned out to be the wealthy and the powerful who fostered a system of negligence and oppression and who refused to repent. Jesus warned the entire generation that they would be destroyed if they did not repent (13:1–5). He commissioned the disciples to preach the message of repentance and forgiveness to all the Gentile nations (24:47). In Luke, Jesus calls *all people* to repentance: the wealthy give up their wealth, the powerful express compassion, tax collectors stop extorting money, prostitutes repent of their sin, and disciples confess their lack of faith.

For Luke, repentance and forgiveness involve a magnificent transformation of the whole person. Luke's story demonstrates how forgiveness results in love, generosity, joy, peace, and perseverance. Some of the most beautiful stories in the Bible are Luke's accounts of the transformation of people experiencing repentance and forgiveness: the prodigal son returns after reaching the end of his rope (15:11–32); Peter recognizes his sinfulness in response to an unexpected catch of fish (5:1–11); Zacchaeus is moved to generosity by Jesus' willingness to enter his unclean house (19:1–10); the prostitute is overwhelmed by gratitude at Jesus' acceptance of her (7:36–50). Sometimes repentance precedes forgiveness. At other times acceptance and forgiveness come first and then evoke repentance. Repentance rids one of priorities other than God. Forgiveness grants one an experience of God's mercy. And the resulting change of behavior has enormous consequences for the life of the nation.

In Luke's second volume, the Acts of the Apostles, we see confirmed Luke's understanding of the means to putting God first—the power of the Holy Spirit. In the last words of Luke's Gospel, the risen Jesus promises the disciples that they will be "clothed with power from on high" (24:49). At the beginning of Acts, the disciples do nothing until the Holy Spirit comes upon them (Acts 1:4–8). Throughout Acts, whenever people repent and are baptized, they are anointed with the Holy Spirit. This is the same Spirit that inspired those who celebrated the birth of John and of Jesus, the Spirit that came upon Jesus after his baptism (3:21–23) and that empowered him for the messianic task (4:18). The distinguishing mark of the Holy Spirit for Luke is compassionate power. And this power orients one to God, most evident in the fact that those who receive the Holy Spirit praise God with expressions of great joy and with speaking in tongues (Acts 2:1–13).

It is this Holy Spirit orienting one to a compassionate God that enables the social inequities to be redressed with mercy. Despite the failure of Israel as a whole to respond favorably to Jesus' message, God's purposes will not be thwarted. For Luke, the early Christian community becomes the locus where Jesus' vision for the political life of the nation is lived out. In this new community, people sell or contribute their possessions and distribute the proceeds according to the needs of people (Acts 2:42–47; 4:32–37). The minority group of Hellenistic Judeans is given authority over the daily distribution of food to assure that also their widows will be cared for (Acts 6:1–7). There is a unity to the group that counters strife. There is a spirit of mutuality among them whereby the leaders serve. People are healed, demons are driven out, the dead are raised. The community is open to all—Judeans, Samaritans, and a whole host of diverse Gentile nations (Acts 10:1–48). And the followers of Jesus boldly proclaim the word, enduring persecution without perpetrating violence. In Luke's vision, this early community is the true expression of God's people, the locus of God's spreading rule on earth, because the Spirit is in charge liberating and empowering people to live the vision of "the things that make for peace" (Luke 19:42).

Lukan Trajectories

The trajectories of the Gospel of Luke have, for the most part, gone in two different directions. One trajectory is the church's commitment to transform society, a prophetic concern for the poor, the oppressed, the widows and orphans, the ill, the aged, and those with disabilities. Here is the social gospel, the visionary effort to bring the kingdom of God to fruition in society. The Society of Saint Luke expresses the church's concern for the sick and infirmed. John Wesley was greatly influenced by Luke in establishing the Methodist movement. Particularly relevant is Wesley's persistent call for the wealthy (all who have any more than enough!) to share their possessions. The United Church of Christ has had a strong commitment to social justice on the Lukan model. The United States Roman Catholic Bishops have issued statements warning of the threats that will come from the growing neglect of the under-class and advocating for society to act on "God's preferential option for the poor." Lukan societal concerns are also represented in contemporary periodicals like *Sojourners*.

More recent are the liberation movements, which draw especially on the Gospel of Luke—the liberation theologies of Central and South America, the freedom movements of South Africa, and the civil rights struggles in the United States for African Americans, Hispanic Americans, Asian Americans, and Native Americans. In this regard, Jesus' inaugural speech in Nazareth declaring "good news to the poor" is one of the most frequently cited biblical passages in the liberation movements. Also, women of many ethnic groups draw upon Luke, because Luke is the Gospel that offers the most extensive treatment of women as followers of Jesus.[2]

The other trajectory is the lively expression of the Holy Spirit as power. This trajectory is manifested mainly in the Pentecostal churches and in the charismatic renewal within the mainline churches. Here is the experience of the Spirit of God as the compassionate power to heal the sick, to drive out demons, and to transform people so that they are oriented to God. With the lively experience of the Spirit come spontaneous expressions of joy in worship—praise, speaking in tongues, singing, and dance. In the contemporary age, testimonies suggest that prayers for the power of the Holy Spirit have liberated people from drug and alcohol addictions, transformed people who are mean and selfish, and led many to do extraordinary acts of kindness and love.

For Luke, these two streams of tradition were one. The same Holy Spirit transforming individuals also empowered people and nations to seek to transform society with mercy. For Luke, social justice and the Spirit of God belong together, for there can be no lasting social justice without the power of the Spirit, and there can be no meaningful life of the Spirit without the manifestation of compassion in society.

Example of a Lukan Community

A contemporary community based on Luke's vision of the gospel would be rooted in a profound experience of God's compassion. Out of the compassion of the Spirit, this community would be committed to oppose all forms of injustice in the society. They would expose the economic forces at work against the poor. They would expose the dynamics of oppression and seek to remove all blocks to compassion for the marginalized. The community would identify the vulnerable members of society around them and then work and advocate on their behalf. Members would seek innovative solutions to societal problems, forged out of compassion. The community would seek to be an embodiment of God's new world in its own life together in the present. They would reflect the universality of the gospel with people from many races, ethnic groups, walks of life, and social classes. Gatherings would be marked by healings, the sharing of resources with the needy, and celebration with a meal. Worship would be marked by joy and praise, with singing, dancing, and praying in the Spirit. Participants would be anointed with the power of the Holy Spirit to carry out courageous acts of compassion for the poor and the oppressed.

Notes

1. In this chapter, the translations are based on the New Revised Standard Version.

2. However, Luke is a two-edged sword in its treatment of women. Luke highlights the presence of women more extensively than the other Gospels, yet he seems to limit the roles of women in the church. See the book by Turid Karlsen Seim.

Further Reading

Boff, Leonardo and Clodovis Boff. *Introducing Liberation Theology.* Maryknoll: Orbis, 1986.

Brawley, Robert. *Centering on God: Method and Message in Luke-Acts.* Louisville: Westminster/John Knox, 1990.

Brown, Robert McAfee. *Liberation Theology: An Introductory Guide.* Louisville: Westminster/John Knox, 1993.

_____. *Unexpected News: Reading the Bible with Third World Eyes.* Philadelphia: Westminster, 1984.

Caird, G. B. *The Gospel of Luke.* Penguin Books, 1963.

Chomsky, Noam. *The Prosperous Few and the Restless Many.* Berkeley: Odonian Press, 1993.

Danker, Frederick. *Jesus and the New Age: A Commentary of St. Luke's Gospel.* Philadelphia: Fortress Press, 1988.

_____. *Luke.* 2d edition, Proclamation Commentaries. Philadelphia: Fortress Press, 1987.

Gutiérrez, Gustavo. *The God of Life*. Maryknoll: Orbis, 1989.

_____. *An Introduction to Liberation Theology*. Maryknoll: Orbis, 1990.

Hanks, Thomas. *God So Loved the Third World: The Bible, the Reformation, and Liberation Theologies*. Maryknoll: Orbis, 1989.

Jennings, Theodore. *Good News to the Poor: John' Wesley's Evangelical Economics*. Nashville: Abingdon, 1990.

Juel, Donald. *Luke-Acts: The Promise of History*. Atlanta: John Knox Press, 1984.

Kingsbury, Jack Dean. *Conflict in Luke: Jesus, Authorities, Disciples*. Minneapolis: Fortress Press, 1991.

Moxnes, Halvor. *The Economy of the Kingdom: Social Conflict and Economic Relations in Luke's Gospel*. Philadelphia: Fortress Press, 1988.

Newsom, Carol and Sharon Ringe, editors. *The Women's Bible Commentary*. Louisville: Westminster/John Knox, 1992.

Parenti, Michael. *Democracy for the Few*. 6th edition. New York: St. Martin's Press, 1995.

Pilgrim, Walter. *Good News to the Poor: Wealth and Poverty in Luke-Acts*. Minneapolis: Augsburg, 1981.

Pobee, John and Barbel von Wartenberg-Potter, editors. *New Eyes for Reading: Biblical and Theological Reflections by Women from the Third World*. Minneapolis: Meyer-Stone, 1986.

Powell, Mark. *What Are They Saying about Luke?* Mahwah, N.J.: Paulist, 1990.

Reimer, Ivoni Richter. *Women in the Acts of the Apostles*. Minneapolis: Fortress Press, 1995.

Ringe, Sharon. *Jesus, Liberation, and the Biblical Jubilee: Images for Ethics and Christology*. Philadelphia: Fortress Press, 1985.

Russell, Letty, editor. *Feminist Interpretation of the Bible*. Philadelphia: Westminster, 1985.

Seim, Turid Karlsen. *The Double-Message: Patterns of Gender in Luke-Acts*. Edinburgh: T. & T. Clark, 1994.

Talbert, Charles. *Reading Luke*. New York: Crossroad, 1982.

Tannehill, Robert. *The Narrative Unity of Luke-Acts*. Volume 1. Philadelphia: Fortress Press, 1986.

Tiede, David L. *Luke*. Minneapolis: Augsburg, 1988.

Wallis, James. *The Soul of Politics: A Practical and Prophetic Vision for Change*. New York: New Press, 1994.

6

The Gospel of John
Eternal Life in the Present

Background and Purpose

JOHN WAS THE LAST OF THE CANONICAL GOSPELS to be written, probably penned near the end of the first century between 90 and 100 C.E. Scholars suggest a variety of locations from which the Gospel might have originated—Alexandria in Egypt, Palestine, Antioch of Syria, or Asia Minor. Asia Minor seems to be a likely location, possibly in the city of Ephesus. The Gospel states that the author is the "disciple whom Jesus loved" (21:20–24). This disciple is never named, but many have conjectured that it is John the son of Zebedee (James and John the sons of Zebedee are not otherwise referred to in this Gospel). Regardless of the identification of the beloved disciple, it is very unlikely that a disciple of Jesus wrote this Gospel, for it was probably written about seventy years after the death of Jesus. Some scholars think that John the son of Zebedee really was behind the traditions in the Gospel and was perhaps part of the community in earlier stages of its life but that he did not write the Gospel. In any case, it was probably a later writer, now unknown to us, who wrote the Gospel of John as we know it today. We will continue to refer to the author as "John." Because this Gospel expresses some themes similar to those in the epistles of John and suggests some connections with the book of Revelation, scholars have conjectured that the author of John was part of a Christian "school" of writers.

We are unsure whether the Gospel was written to a community of people with Judean background or Gentile background. The Gospel may have emerged out of a conflict with other Christians. At one time, some community members may have been part of a synagogue but had been expelled or excommunicated from the

Jewish synagogues for their Christian beliefs (9:22; 12:42). The author wrote to strengthen and solidify the life and beliefs of Christians in the face of conflict and persecution. We can infer that the life of the Christian community of this Gospel was spiritually oriented. Participants believed that Jesus was alive among them and continued to speak in their midst, probably through prophets and other members of the community. Participants apparently had such a rich and meaningful relationship with the risen Jesus that they believed eternal life—full, abundant life in the Spirit—was already accessible to them in the present. As such, this community was composed of people who shared a common spiritual relationship with God through Jesus and had developed their own metaphorical language—life, light, bread, living water, and so on—as a means to convey to others the depth and meaning of their experience as Christians. In sharing this experience together, members probably expressed great love for each other.

The Gospel of John is quite different from the other three canonical Gospels. Consider, for example, the following features that are unique or distinctive in the Gospel of John: the origins of Jesus are traced back to God's act of creation; Jesus proclaims his identity openly and is acknowledged as Son of God by many; Jesus speaks in long monologues, often structured around sayings about himself that begin with the words "I am . . ."; these monologues are replete with symbolic language; Jesus has numerous conversations with characters who misunderstand his symbolic language; Jesus offends and alienates many people by his claim to be equal with God; Jesus does seven miracles, called signs; there are no exorcisms; there is almost no ethical teaching as we see in Matthew; there is no emphasis on social justice as we see in Luke; the cleansing of the temple occurs at the beginning of the story; during his public ministry, Jesus goes often to Jerusalem; there are characters who do not appear in other Gospels, such as Nicodemus, the Samaritan woman, the man born blind, and Lazarus, among others; at the Passover meal, Jesus washes the disciples' feet; the first disciples come to Jesus from John; many disciples stop following Jesus because his sayings are offensive; there is an enigmatic "disciple whom Jesus loved"; Jesus' death is depicted as a glorification; the resurrection stories include unique episodes about Mary Magdalene, Thomas, and Peter; and, at the end, the narrator explains why he has written the Gospel.[1]

The Two Ways: Not Knowing God or Knowing God

Writ large in the Gospel of John is a cosmic and experiential dualism, characterized by the polarities of light and dark, above and below, Spirit and flesh, life and death, truth and falsehood, heaven and earth, God and Satan. The dualism is cosmic; that is, it reflects the realities of the universe. The dualism is also experiential; that is, it depicts two different ways of experiencing life, two different ways of being in the world, two different self–understandings. Now this is a distinctive dualism. Many New Testament writings project salvation or punishment into the future, heaven above or hell below. John's world has two choices now—life or death, light or darkness, God or Satan—two possibilities that exist now in this life. John makes little distinction between now and later— between now and after one dies or between now and in some new age. The two possibilities confront people fully now in the present moment.

The plot of John's Gospel is that God loved the world so much that God acted to restore an alienated creation to full relationship with its creator. God had created the world through the Word, but the world had become estranged from God. So now God took the creative "word" and enfleshed this word as human being, Jesus of Nazareth. God commissioned Jesus to manifest the reality of God and to bring life to the world, so that those who believe in him would have eternal life in a restored relationship with the creator and with creation. God has commissioned Jesus with authority for salvation and judgment (5:26–27). No one has ever seen God except the Son, and Jesus the Son has come to make God known (1:18).

John's Gospel tells how Jesus manifests God to a series of people or groups. The narrative depicts these manifestations in a series of dramatic encounters between Jesus and another character, encounters that bring the true nature of the characters to light. The narrative of each encounter is quite extended, especially when compared with the brief stories in the other Gospels. Often, the narratives contain lengthy monologues of Jesus or dialogues between characters, as in a play,

In these narratives, the characters are defined by their relationship with Jesus. Jesus was sent from God, but he is not recognized as one sent from God except by a few. He comes to his own, but his own do not receive him (1:11). The light shines in darkness;

nevertheless, the darkness does not comprehend the light (1:5). Most people reject Jesus—which *is* the judgment against them. These are the authorities in Israel, who put Jesus on trial by question and accusation throughout the story. Jesus defends himself by the witness of scripture, miraculous signs, and his own words. Eventually, the authorities put him to death. A few people, however, discern that Jesus is sent from God—which *is* the salvation for them (3:16–21). These people are Jesus' disciples, friends such as Mary and Martha and Lazarus and other people who believe in him. The Gospel narratives portray the process whereby people choose one or the other of these two responses to Jesus.

The two possibilities confront people now in the present moment. The following chart sets out the characteristics of the two ways:

Not Knowing God	*Knowing God*
Alienated from God	Abiding in God
Death	(Eternal) Life
Darkness	Light
Born once	Born also from above
Oriented to flesh	Oriented to Spirit
Mundane existence	Spiritual existence
Living a lie	Doing the Truth
Seeking one's own glory	Seeking God's glory
Immorality (murderers)	Morality (losing life for a friend)
Judgment (even now)	Salvation (even now)

As we have indicated, John's dualism may have emerged from a social situation in the late first century somewhere outside of Palestine where a Christian group was involved in conflicts with other groups, including a situation in which it was no longer possible for Christians to worship in synagogues because of the reactions to the claims they as Christians were making about Jesus. These Christians were probably isolated and alienated from the world around them. Their rich spiritual experience of the risen Jesus and the solidarity of their community probably made them aware of how different they were from the rest of the world. Persecution likely polarized this experience into "us" and "them"; we insiders who are open to the truth and those outsiders who are willfully blind; we who are in the light and they who are in darkness; we who have abundant life and they, the living dead; we who know reality and they who live a lie; we who are reborn of Spirit and they who are limited to the mundane perspective of the flesh.

Because of the polarizing nature of John's worldview, it is appropriate again to sound a reminder about anti-Judaism. The Gospel of John is built on a dualism of cosmic proportions. John associates Jesus with the positive side of the dualism, replacing the whole legal foundation of Judaism with another foundation. John associates "the Judeans" with the negative side of the dualism, with "the world," evil, darkness, Satan, slavery, and judgment. John tends to lump together under the single category of "Judeans" those people who do not believe in Jesus, who slander and then execute him. By calling the leaders who executed Jesus generically as "Judeans" rather than distinguishing them as Pharisees or Sadducees or elders, John's language implies that Judeans as a whole were opposed to Jesus. As with the other Gospels, this stereotypical characterization of Judean opponents of Jesus is used for rhetorical purposes to characterize the opposite of Jesus. However, even though John's "Judeans" can be viewed as "symbolic" of all who do not accept Jesus, the term nevertheless has a clear anti-Judean thrust. When Christianity became a powerful force, these depictions especially contributed to the persecution of Jews by Christians.

The Human Condition: Not Knowing God Is Death

The basic human condition in John's Gospel is that characters generally are limited to the mundane realm of the flesh because they do not "know" God; that is, they have no spiritual knowledge of God (8:47). Being in the dark, limited to a mundane understanding of things, the characters have difficulty grasping the realm that Jesus shows them. The result is a series of dialogues of misunderstanding in which Jesus speaks to others about the spiritual realm. However, they simply do not get what he is talking about: Nicodemus thinks "born again" means entering the mother's womb (3:4); the woman at the well thinks "living water" is running water (4:1–15); the Judean leaders think the temple refers only to the complex of buildings in Jerusalem (2:19–22); the crowd in the desert cannot understand how Jesus was bread to eat (6:43–59); people think Jesus' talk about his Father refers to his father of lineage (8:14–19); the Jewish leaders confuse Jesus' reference to freedom with liberation from slavery (8:31–38); Mary assumes that resurrection is only a future reality (11:21–27); the disciples think Jesus is going on a trip when he talks about being "the way" (14:1–6); Pilate supposes Jesus' kingdom had its origin in this world (18:35–37); and so on. It is necessary for Jesus to speak in symbolic ways, because his words are revealing the reality of God—and we can only speak about God in symbolic language. While a few characters move on to understand this reality, most people are unable to comprehend his language as symbolic and metaphorical—because they do not "know" the realm or dimension of reality to which the metaphors refer, namely, the reality of God.

Being limited to a grasp of only transitory, mundane things—the temple will fall, the water will leave one thirsty again, the bread will go stale, a kingdom will fall—the people who do not understand are themselves thereby transitory, mortal, temporal, subject to death. They are transitory, because they have no relationship with that which is eternal, that which does not perish, that which endures (3:16). Because they do not drink the water of life, they will drink and be thirsty again (4:13–14). Because they do not consume heavenly bread, they will eat bread and die (6:48–51). Thus, the human condition is that, apart from being in relationship with God, people are subject to death. Therefore, those who do not come into relationship with God through Jesus (those who do not know God) are condemned already because they do not pass from death into life (5:24), and they will die in their sin (8:21). In John, sin is equivalent to "not believing in Jesus," that is, not knowing the eternal God (17:3). That *is* the judgment: not knowing God now, not being related to what is eternal now, people will simply die. If they do not have life in relation to God, they will perish (10:28). "For God so loved the world that he gave his only Son, so that everyone who believes in him may not *perish* but may have eternal life" (3:16). The choices are not future realities of heaven or hell but present realities of lasting life in relation to the eternal God or death.

In John's Gospel, the focus is not on ethics but on knowing or not knowing God; nevertheless, morality and the lack of morality are wedded to these two experiences. In John's view, life lived outside a relationship with God will be immoral. When the light shines in darkness those who are evil will avoid the light, because the light exposes their deeds. They love darkness rather than light because their deeds are evil (3:19–20). Thus, those who do not come to know God in Jesus are people who seek their own glory rather than God's glory, have no love in themselves, lack compassion, lie (8:55), show an unwillingness to die for a friend (10:12), entertain a murderous intent against those who threaten their world (8:42–44), and offer leadership that is destructive (10:1–18). Otherwise, they would be drawn to the light—to God in Jesus (3:21). But they are children of Satan (8:44). And in their darkness, without knowledge of God, they are blind to their true nature. As with salvation and judgment, morality and immorality are intrinsic to the very experience of knowing or not knowing God, who is love. Whether or not one knows God—that is crucial. And the basic human condition is that generally people do not know God.

The Vision for Human Life: Knowing God Is Eternal Life

The goal of God in the narrative world is the same as the stated purpose of John's Gospel. The Gospel was written, the author asserts, "so that you may come to believe that Jesus is the Messiah, the Son of God, and that through believing you may have life in his name" (20:31). The goal of the Gospel is that the reader might have life, and when John is talking about life, he means eternal life—rich, full, abundant life. "I came," Jesus says, "that you may have life, and have it abundantly" (10:10). We may be misled by the translation "eternal life" into thinking that the primary focus of John's treatment of life is that it lasts forever. That is certainly a dimension of John's understanding of eternal life, for someone who has eternal life will, in some sense, never die (11:26). However, the primary focus of John's understanding of eternal life is on the quality of that life—the depth, the meaning, the fullness of "eternal life." Just because life lasts forever does not mean that it is fulfilling. What if we lived forever but were bored to tears? The issue for John is the fullness of life in personal relation with God, because the intimate experience of knowing God is transforming and humanly fulfilling. For John, this relationship with God is available in the present, and therefore eternal life is available in the present.

John's view of eternal life is explicitly defined in the narrative world by Jesus: "And this is eternal life, that they may know you, the only true God, and Jesus Christ whom you have sent" (17:3). Eternal life is the mystical relationship with God, the very experience of knowing God, who is fully revealed through the Son Jesus. For the writer of John, eternal life is a profoundly spiritual experience, so profound that the author is led to make a sharp distinction between Spirit and flesh. Spirit gives birth to Spirit; flesh gives birth to flesh (3:5–8). The Spirit (of God) brings life; the flesh avails for nothing. Being born of the Spirit is to enter the life of God. And the new life made available by the Spirit is the personal experience of knowing God.

John's dualism is a dualism of orientation or direction or stance. As such, the orientation to the Spirit involves an opposition to darkness and Satan, but it is not an opposition to flesh or world or earth *as such*. Flesh, world, and earth were created by God. Apart from God, they can be evil. Yet, restored to God, they can be redeemed. One is born of Spirit and can still remain in the flesh—without being oriented to the flesh. One can abide in God and still remain in the world—without being oriented to the world. One can be part of a kingdom originating from heaven and still remain on earth—without being oriented to an earthly kingdom. God created all of life and seeks to deliver people out of alienation from God to a restored relationship of creation with God. John's theology is not a denial of the goodness of flesh, life, the world, the earth, but an affirmation of its fulfillment when people know God and abide in relationship with God through the Spirit.

Knowing God is the experience of a whole new dimension of life—so strange and new and rich that it requires a new vocabulary and new meanings to old words: one must be born from above, of the Spirit (3:5); streams of living water will flow from one's heart to quench forever one's thirst for life (4:13–15; 7:38); Jesus is to be ingested as bread from heaven to satisfy forever one's hunger for fulfillment (6:51); Jesus is the light that illuminates the world as never before (3:21; 8:12); Jesus is the resurrection—and a relationship with Jesus enables one to experience resurrection life now (11:25). Other terms have appropriately distinctive meanings. In this Gospel, "truth" is not accurate information; it is God's reality. "Believing" in Jesus is not affirming a proposition; it is being open to relationship with God in Jesus (and faith is always a verb in John). "Knowing God" is not a matter of having knowledge about God; it is having an intimate personal relationship with the source of life (17:3).

The depiction of this new relationship offered in John is delivered from generalities and abstractions; all of it is made personal by being equated with the person Jesus. He is the word, the truth, the life, the way, the resurrection, the light, the bread, the living water, the gate, the good shepherd, the vine, the temple. He is life, and to know God through Jesus is eternal life. Every word, concept, idea, is transformed in light of the new reality experienced in Jesus. In this Gospel, Jesus does not institute the sacraments of bread and wine, as if to say that bread and wine are not the only vehicles of the special presence of God. In John's Gospel, *every* ordinary thing in the created order that is vital to life points beyond itself to the reality of the one who created it. Birth, bread, water, light, and so on are sacralized in the service of bringing people to know God through Jesus. Indeed all places and all times of creation are sacralized as potential vehicles of the reality of God, as signs bearing the presence of the creator, as means to know God.

This experience of knowing God is deeply moral, because it involves intimate knowledge of the God who is love (14:21). As evil behavior is associated with not knowing God, so a moral life is inherent in the experience of knowing God. In John, the love of others does not focus on enemies or outsiders but occurs among the committed relationships of the community members who know God. To be sure, the believers are to reflect the God who "so loved the (whole) world"; nevertheless, the focus is on the community. The community of believers is set apart by their love for one another, their willingness to die for a friend, as the good shepherd lays down his life for his sheep (15:12–17). Those who respond favorably to Jesus do not fear the light (3:21). They are drawn to the light, which reveals that their works are good. They are people who seek the glory of God rather than their own glory (7:18). In relation to Jesus, they bear fruit, just as branches that draw nourishment from the vine bear fruit (15:1–8). By their example, the community models the relationships among God's creatures as they were meant to be.

In John's world, the belief in Jesus and the spiritual experience of knowing God go hand in hand; whoever believes has "passed from death to life" and "has eternal life" (5:24). We need to be cautious not to reduce John's understanding of the Christian life to our own experience. We live in a world where people grow up believing in Jesus and where believing in Jesus can mean little or nothing. Often the act of believing in Jesus is not correlated in any way with spiritual experience. However, John apparently lived in a world where those who became Christians experienced a radical transformation. Believing in Jesus, coming into relationship with God through Jesus, entailed a whole new way of seeing the world, and that transformation in seeing triggered a profoundly mystical relationship with God. This is why Jesus' very words *are* "eternal life" (5:24; 7:63–68)—because they are a vehicle for the experience of God. Recognizing God in Jesus and experiencing God in a spiritual way occur simultaneously. Recognizing God in Jesus was for John's community, therefore, an experience in which the Spirit flowed within them like streams of living water (7:38). This mystical relationship with God *is* the salvation of eternal life that delivers one from the sinful mundane existence of not knowing God.

In depicting John's idea of eternal life as a "mystical" relationship, I mean a transformative knowing of reality that comes from being in unity with God. It is not a rational, informational knowing about God but an existential awareness of profound fulfillment. John uses symbols of deep meaning, of nourishment, of glory, and of illumination to convey this mystical awareness. John's spirituality is not a mysticism whereby one ascends by meditation and discipline up a ladder to higher enlightenment. Rather, John's mystical knowing is given as gift in the act of believing in(to) Jesus. Nor is John's spirituality a mysticism of union with the divine whereby one's identity is lost in an oceanic experience of divine reality. Rather, the person's identity is preserved through a mutual "abiding in," whereby the believer abides in God and God abides in the believer. There is a mutual participation in the life of the other without absorption. Nor is this a mystical unity with all of life. Rather, John focuses on believers in unity with one another as they abide in Jesus and Jesus abides in God. By abiding in the creator, the believers also come into harmony with the creation, which now bears witness everywhere as a cornucopia of symbols to the nature of this unity with God.

Furthermore, John's mysticism is not a static union of just

"being" in a relationship with God. Rather, it is a dynamic unity in harmony with God's will and action. The believer comes into harmony with God's active love, just as Jesus manifested God's work in his work and God's glory in his self-giving death. This love is expressed in the concrete action of mutual footwashing whereby believers become a part of Jesus and of one another (13:1–20). Finally, John's mysticism may have involved either momentary mystical "experiences" or an enduring mystical awareness. In any case, the focus is on the human fulfillment that comes in the relationship with God through Jesus. The intimacy of knowing God is profoundly expressed when Jesus refers to those who follow him as his "friends" (15:14–15).

In John's Gospel, this experience of eternal life is fully accessible in the present, because the experience of knowing God is fully available through Jesus (17:3). In John, eternal life is not something that will be experienced only after death, nor is it something that believers only taste in this life with a fuller experience to come after death or in a new age. Eternal life is fully accessible now, even in the midst of vicissitudes and persecutions, because the relationship with God is fully accessible now through Jesus. It is true that John sometimes adds at the end of a declaration about eternal life, "and I will raise them up on the last day" (6:40). But there is no indication that this adds anything to the present quality of eternal life in relation to God through Jesus. Every theological concept— judgment, salvation, belief, death, eternal life—is brought to bear upon present possibilities in a thoroughgoing way. The author of John's Gospel and his community have apparently had such a rich and profound experience of the risen living Jesus that they were moved to affirm: This is it! This is eternal life! And the goal of God and of Jesus in the story world and the purpose of the author in writing the gospel is for people to have this eternal life (20:31).

The importance of John's Gospel for contemporary life is fairly obvious. We live in a culture that is not conducive to spirituality. Whether we are poor and struggling or well-off and secure, the demands and pace of life generally do not lend themselves to a nurturing of the spiritual quality in our lives. Many people, including single parents, must work several jobs in order to get by. Often the work itself deadens the human spirit. Many companies reward a workaholic devotion to the job. Members of families are often overcommitted in many different directions. Leisure time, television, and popular entertainment are often simply superficial, temporary escapes from the stresses of life. Furthermore, most of our lives are spent in an urban world of buildings and pavements tragically separated from the rest of creation.

It is clear that there is a search for spiritual meaning and fulfillment by many people today. The success of the New Age movement attests to that. Many self-help books emphasize the importance of meditation for mental and physical health. Christians may turn to their churches for meaning in life. Unfortunately, many Christians do not find spiritual depth and vitality in their churches. Often, people are Christians because their parents were Christians, without having claimed the faith for themselves through a spiritual experience of God. Many Christians attend church with little commitment to Jesus in their lives, because they have never been grasped by the Spirit of God in their hearts and souls. At the same time, many churches do nurture a deep spirituality, and many of these churches find the Gospel of John to be a rich source for spiritual life and personal renewal.

The Gospel of John proclaims a profound human experience of the creator of all things. It is not a vague ethereal spirituality, but one that claims the immense love of God in the historical figure of Jesus, whose death and resurrection opened the way for human beings to gain access to a renewing energy at the heart of the universe. John's spirituality does not seek to make people divine, but rather offers a fulfilling relation with the divine that makes human life full and rich and enduring. John's spirituality is not a spirituality that is an end in itself, but one that draws the transformed believers into the flow of God's love for one another and for the world. The presence of John's gospel in the canon is a crucial witness to an expression of Christianity with profound spiritual depths.

The Transformation: Union with Jesus Made Possible by His Death and the Presence of the Holy Spirit

How is the world restored to an intimate relationship with God? How do we create communities of love? Here the key question is this: How does someone go from the realm of darkness to the spiritual experience of eternal life?

For John, this is possible through Jesus. Jesus originates from heaven, from above, where God dwells. He has seen God and is sent by God to manifest God to the world. Jesus is the definitive agent of God to bear God's reality to the world. Jesus is the audible, visible, and obtainable manifestation of God in the world. His words and actions are expressions of the will of the One who sent him. To hear Jesus' words is to hear God's words. To see Jesus' actions is to see God's actions. Jesus' key role is to reveal the Father. Thus, to be open to the reality of Jesus is to be open to the reality of God. That is, Jesus leads people to have faith in him and by being in relation with him to have eternal life, and this eternal life *is* their salvation. Jesus also comes for judgment, because if people reject him they remain in the realm of darkness and death, and this rejection *is* their judgment. In every encounter, Jesus seeks to draw people into belief and a positive response. Jesus presses the issue until there is either a positive response or an explicit rejection. And once people have encountered Jesus and in that encounter seen God, they no longer have any excuse for their blindness.

It is not clear in John's world why some people respond and others do not. On the one hand, only those whom God draws will believe (6:65). And yet in his death, Jesus is "drawing all people" to himself (12:32). In some cases, people recognize Jesus because they already know God just by being the type of persons they are. Nathanael, for example, is without guile and readily discerns that Jesus is God's Son (1:43–50). Other people resist Jesus because their deeds are evil. Yet, the woman at the well, who is a Samaritan and who has had five husbands and now lives with one who is not her husband, comes to believe Jesus is the Messiah (5:39–42). People who know that the Scriptures speak of Jesus may come to believe. Others may respond to the miraculous signs (2:23). People do not come to Jesus unless in some way they are drawn, yet they also choose their response.

Different characters in the story are at different stages of positive or negative responses to Jesus. Jesus seeks to move each character toward one choice or the other. In the Gospel narrative, the first step toward a commitment to Jesus is a positive encounter with Jesus, then belief in him as God's Son and an acceptance of what he says, which in turn includes an openness to experiencing the reality of God that Jesus manifests.

There are people in John's story who come to believe in Jesus, and yet they do not yet seem to have experienced eternal life. The reason for this is that the Gospel depicts a period of time before the Spirit has come to believers. Not until the Spirit is available do the believers actually experience eternal life in a spiritual way. As long as Jesus is the word incarnate in human reality, Jesus cannot manifest himself as Spirit. That is, believers cannot encounter God as Spirit until Jesus is transformed into a spiritual reality.

But how does the concrete human Jesus become available to the believer as a spiritual reality? The death and resurrection of Jesus and the consequent presence of the Spirit make this possible. Jesus is the lamb of God who takes away the sin of the world. In John's view, sin is the lack of intimate knowledge of God. By his death, Jesus makes that intimate knowing available spiritually (7:38–39). The death of Jesus enables his own relationship with God to be possible for others: "Unless a grain of wheat falls into the earth and dies, it remains just a single grain; but if it dies, it bears much fruit" (12:24). Only if Jesus dies and goes to the Father can Jesus establish for believers the same relation to God that he has. In John's Gospel, there is no real suffering for Jesus on the cross, nor is there a humiliation and subsequent exaltation. Rather, Jesus is a majestic figure whose death is itself an exaltation, because it is the means by which he acts to become spiritually available to those who believe in him. This self-sacrifice for others is the supreme manifestation of God's love for the world.

Thus, the well-known passage we often hear at funerals refers not to a life in heaven after death but to the life available to believers here after Jesus' death. "In my Father's house are many dwelling [abiding] places. . . . And if I go and prepare a place for you I will *come again* and will take you to myself, so that where I am, there you may be also" (14:1–5). The Father's house is the temple, and Jesus' resurrected body is the new temple (2:21). As a result of Jesus' death and resurrection, the new temple, Jesus' body, becomes spiritually available to believers as the abiding place where they worship God, neither in Jerusalem nor on Mount Gerizim, but in spirit and in truth (4:21–24). Abiding in Jesus as Jesus abides in God *is* the place Jesus prepares for them. Thus, for John, the "second coming" takes place immediately after Jesus' death when the living Jesus returns in spiritual form through the presence of the Spirit. Jesus died to secure that place; he comes back through the Spirit, the "comforter" (14:26), and receives believers to himself so that where he is, namely, abiding in God, they too might be, by abiding in him. And this relation with God, this intimate knowledge of God made available through Jesus, is the experience of eternal life that endures forever.

By means of Jesus' death and resurrection, the mystical unity of the believer with God is made available (7:38). The Spirit testifies to Jesus by being the vehicle for his reality. The Spirit brings life, and Jesus is the life. John uses the metaphor of "abiding" to articulate the unity of the believer with the Father made possible by the Spirit. Jesus says: "I am in my Father, and you in me, and I in you" (14:20), "We will come to them and make our home in them" (14:23), and "That they may be one, as we are one" (17:22). In this unity, the joy and peace of Jesus are present (20:19–21). In this unity, the believer is a child of God by virtue of having the same relationship with God that the son Jesus has with the Father (1:12–13). In this unity, all of life breathes a restored creation.

The very presence and rich spiritual life of John's community apparently served as witness to the truth and reality of what they believed. John wrote to strengthen that community and its experience of the risen Jesus. In this regard, John's community probably did not see itself as a mission community sent out on journeys to reach the whole world. In the Gospel, there is a sending out of the disciples and a commissioning of apostles, but John's community likely witnessed primarily by its presence in the world. The disciples are sent to witness as Jesus has witnessed, with words that bear eternal life. The author wrote, in part, so that others who have not seen may "believe that Jesus is the Messiah, the Son of God, and that through believing you may have life in his name" (20:31). Jesus' words are words of life, because the believing of the words brings the experience of the eternal life to which the words witness.

Because the narrative conveys the words of Jesus, the Gospel itself becomes the "words of eternal life"! In this way, the narrative leads hearers to the experience of eternal life. Perhaps the author hoped that the hearers would identify with the different characters at various stages of response to Jesus and thereby be drawn into believing in Jesus. And the author may have hoped by means of the repeated dialogues of misunderstanding to draw the hearer into greater (in)sight than the uncomprehending characters in the story and thereby draw the hearer into an experience of the divine reality. For the hearer, there is an accumulative impact to this new language—you must be born again, no, not in the womb, but born of Spirit; living water, no, not running water, but water that wells up into eternal life; bread, no, not perishable bread, but bread from heaven; freedom, no, not liberation from slavery, but freedom from the spiritual limitations of the flesh; the way, no, not a road, but an access to the Father; resurrection, no, not at the end, but now, for I am the resurrection and the life. Perhaps at some point in this narrative, the bell will ring, the penny will drop, the light will go on, and the hearer will realize and experience the whole new realm of divine reality to which the narrative points.

How can we today experience John as a Gospel addressed to us? How can the church foster, evoke, nurture, and sustain the spiritual depth of John's religious experience for people in our time? We have much to learn from John, for John's Gospel seeks in many ways to create a renewed relation with the creator and lover of all things: he tells stories about Jesus; he portrays characters who are deadened and characters who are alive with new life; he uses rich imagery and symbolism; he appeals to people's experience of the common things of life; he turns to the concrete experiences of nature as vehicles of the divine; he conveys Jesus' words of promise and assurance; he writes so as to create new life. The church in our day can draw upon John's experience of Jesus and also find new and creative ways to address the problems of our lives so as to bring the kind of spiritual fulfillment to people that will renew both the church and the world in the life of God.

Johannine Trajectories

The trajectories of the Gospel of John are evident wherever there is a lively spiritual experience of Christianity. A survey was recently done of preaching topics in five major Protestant denominations. A study of the sermons collected from numerous pastors revealed that most sermons were on texts from the Gospels, and the Gospel appearing most frequently was John. There are so many rich symbols in John, so many memorable sayings, such a high view of Jesus, such a profound spirituality, that this Gospel has become a favorite across many Christian churches. One of the predominant themes from John that occurs across many traditions, particularly the evangelical traditions, is the spiritual experience of being "born again."

The trajectories of John are also manifest in the areas of mysticism and spirituality. Certainly the monastic traditions of spiritual discipline fall into this category, as do the lively visions and mystical journeys of the saints. To be included is the Eastern Orthodox emphasis upon the transcendent in the ordinary, expressed in the notion of the cosmic Christ, enacted in the dramas of the liturgy, and symbolized in the images of the icons. Modern exercises in guided meditation often draw upon the imagery of John's Gospel. There are also the contemporary reflections of such figures as Thomas Merton, Howard Thurman, Henri Nouwen, Richard Foster, Matthew Fox, as well as the influence of psychologist C. G. Jung. We can also point to the work of Tilden Edwards at the Shalem Institute for Spiritual Formation.

Example of a Johannine Community

An idealized picture of a contemporary community based on John's vision of the gospel would be a place of deep spirituality. Members would be open to knowing God in personal and intimate ways. They would be aware of the many forms of spiritual death in contemporary society and feel their lives had been opened up to a rebirth into God's presence. Their worship would be marked by the use of traditional and contemporary symbols as vehicles of God and of the presence of Jesus. The environment of worship might include architecture, art, and music that awakens the human spirit. The community might foster a ministry in small groups marked by mutual love. Washing of feet would perhaps symbolize their mutual service to each other. They would nurture friendships with Jesus and with one another in the deepest sense of the word. They might also be in close relationship with the natural world as a means to experience the creator. They would draw on many resources to encourage disciplines of prayer and meditation. Their love for each other would overflow into their daily lives, and they would be eager to invite others to "come and see" the love of God through Jesus in their community.

Note

1. The translations in this chapter are based on the New Revised Standard Version.

Further Reading

Brown, Raymond. *The Community of the Beloved Disciple*. New York: Paulist Press, 1979.

Capra, Fritjof. *The Tao of Physics: An Exploration of the Parallels Between Modern Physics and Eastern Mysticism*. 2d edition. New York: Bantam, 1983.

Cassidy, Richard. *John's Gospel in New Perspective*. Maryknoll: Orbis, 1992.

Countryman, William. *The Mystical Way of the Fourth Gospel: Crossing Over into God*. Philadelphia: Fortress Press, 1987.

Culpepper, Alan. *Anatomy of the Fourth Gospel: A Study in Literary Design*. Philadelphia: Fortress Press, 1993.

Edwards, Tilden. *Living in the Presence: Spiritual Exercises to Open Our Lives to the Awareness of God*. San Francisco: Harper, 1987.

Elwood, Robert. *Mysticism and Religion*. Englewood Cliffs: Prentice Hall, 1980.

Fischer, Kathleen. *Women at the Well: Feminist Perspectives on Spiritual Direction*. New York: Paulist, 1988.

Foster, Richard. *Celebration of Disciplines: The Path to Spiritual Growth*. San Francisco: Harper and Row, 1988.

Fox, Matthew. *Original Blessing*. Sante Fe: Bear & Company, 1983.

Karris, Robert. *Jesus and the Marginalized in John's Gospel*. Collegeville: Liturgical Press, 1990.

Koester, Craig. *Symbolism in the Fourth Gospel: Meaning, Mystery, Community*. Minneapolis: Fortress Press, 1995.

Kysar, Robert. *John: The Maverick Gospel*. 2d edition. Louisville: Westminster/John Knox, 1993.

_____. *John*. Minneapolis: Augsburg, 1986.

Lakoff, George and Mark Turner. *More Than Cool Reason: A Field Guide to Poetic Metaphor*. Chicago: University of Chicago Press, 1989.

McDonagh, Sean. *The Greening of the Church*, especially chapter 7. Maryknoll: Orbis, 1990.

MacRae, George. *Invitation to John*. Garden City, N.Y.: Doubleday, 1978.

Moore, Thomas. *The Care of the Soul: A Guide for Cultivating Depth and Sacredness in Everyday Life*. New York: HarperCollins, 1992.

Nash, James. *Loving Nature: Ecological Integrity and Christian Responsibility*. Nashville: Abingdon, 1991.

Nouwen, Henri. *Here and Now: Living in the Spirit*. New York: Crossroad, 1994.

O'Day, Gail. *Revelation in the Fourth Gospel: Narrative Mode and Theological Claim*. Philadelphia: Fortress Press, 1986.

Painter, John. *The Quest for the Messiah: The History, Literature, and Theology of the Johannine Community.* 2d edition. Nashville: Abingdon, 1993.

Peterson, Eugene. *Take & Read. Spiritual Reading: An Annotated List.* Grand Rapids: Eerdmans, 1996.

Rensberger, David. *Johannine Faith and Liberating Community.* Philadelphia: Westminster, 1988.

Robb, Carol and Carl Casebolt, editors. *Covenant for a New Creation: Ethics, Religion, and Public Policy,* especially chapter 4. Maryknoll: Orbis, 1991.

Sanford, John. *Mystical Christianity: A Psychological Commentary on the Gospel of John.* New York: Crossroad, 1993.

Santa-Maria, L. *Growth through Meditation and Journal Writing: A Jungian Perspective on Christian Spirituality,* especially chapter 4. New York: Paulist, 1983.

Scroggs, Robin. *Christology in Paul and John.* Philadelphia: Fortress Press, 1988.

Segovia, Fernando. *The Farewell of the Word: The Johannine Call to Abide.* Minneapolis: Fortress Press, 1991.

Senior, Donald. *The Passion of Jesus in the Gospel of John.* Collegeville: Liturgical Press, 1991.

Smith, Moody. *John.* 2d edition, Proclamation Commentaries. Philadelphia: Fortress Press, 1986.

Talbert, Charles. *Reading John.* New York: Crossroad, 1992.

Thurman, Howard. *Mysticism and the Experience of Love.* Wallingford, Pa.: Pendle Hill, 1961.

Underhill, Evelyn. *Mysticism.* Totawa, N.J.: Rowman and Littlefield, 1977.

7

Reading for Renewal

HERE, THEN, ARE FIVE EXAMPLES OF DIVERSE WORLDVIEWS in the New Testament. These worldviews represent penetrating analyses of our human condition, profound visions of what human life might become, and powerful ways to effect transformation and change. We need all these diverse views and more as resources to address the complex and difficult circumstances in our world today. We could go on to look at other worldviews in the New Testament: the holiness model of 1 Peter, the pilgrimage theology of the letter to the Hebrews, the condemnation of idolatry in the book of Revelation, and the diverse theological perspectives in different Pauline letters. We could also explore the great diversity of smaller traditions that lie embedded within the New Testament writings. All would reinforce the basic notion that in the New Testament canon there are many different ways of viewing the world and of understanding the ways God works to transform the world. So what are we to do with this diversity? How can the diversity challenge and renew us in our life and mission today?

Preserving the Diversity

We may be uncomfortable with the diverse Christian views in the New Testament. We may be uneasy that we cannot settle on one view as the right view. We may want to ask: Which worldview is the correct one? Can I put all these visions together into one scheme? We may feel the psychological need to systematize the diversity or to rank it or to make it all cohere. Nevertheless, we need to learn to keep the diversity so as not to lose it, not to ignore it, not to cover it over, or, as one writer put it, "Not to pretty it up." If we are to get renewal from this diversity, we first need to preserve it, indeed, to guard it.

Human beings have mental filters that tend to eliminate what is disagreeable or does not cohere. A student was upset that Mark's theology did not affirm her view of Jesus, and in exasperation she said, "I'm a Christian and I know what I believe. I don't care what Mark says!" But why would we ever put ourselves into such a mental trap? Why would we think there is only one legitimate way to see things? How could we as human beings believe that we know without doubt what the Christian way is? It may seem "safe" to settle on one point of view as the only one, and it may be threatening to be open to uncertainty, to ambiguity, to paradox, to contradiction, to multiple ways of seeing, but to do so may be much more faithful to the Bible and to the complexities of life.

Once we relinquish the assumption that there is just one legitimate perspective, we can open ourselves to many biblical perspectives about God. In physics it takes two separate models, the wave model and the particle model, to capture all the properties of light. The models are incompatible with each other and cannot be combined into one model. As a result, the two models must be used independently; yet both are necessary to account for all the properties of light. How much more complex the reality of God? How many more models might we need to convey the purposes of God for human beings?

Some psychologists have at hand six or eight models of human behavior and their respective means of therapy—many incompatible with each other—Freudian, behaviorist, transactional, rational-emotive, systems therapy, and so on. One therapist may be familiar with several of these models and then choose one or the other model to use depending on the client or the problem to be treated or the situation to be addressed. Should the understanding of the human condition from a religious point of view or the work of God among us be any less complex?

I was taken aback years ago when a student said to me, "I can't figure out where you're coming from." I realized that I had been teaching each of the writings in the New Testament with such intensity, different though they be, that I presented myself as firmly rooted in all of them. The student could not figure out my preference and wanted to know where *I* was coming from. I was as surprised as the student was to find myself saying, "Actually, I'm coming from a lot of places." As individuals and as groups,

we can embrace multiple perspectives out of the New Testament
without collapsing the diversity and without dissolving the ten-
sions, because we know that truth is more complex and mysteri-
ous than one formulation.

The point is that we come not only to tolerate the diversity in
the New Testament, but that we treasure it and celebrate it as a
means to deepen and renew our lives. Unless we are committed
to taking risks in listening to the biblical writings, we are probably not ready to hear all the good news. Unless we are willing, for
example, to face squarely that in Mark's Gospel God calls people
to endure persecution if necessary for the good news, that in
Luke's Gospel people are called to great compassion for the poor,
and that in John's Gospel full eternal life is accessible now, we
will not get the renewal that is so vital, renewal that can come in
so many different ways. We may not be called as an individual or
as a community to live out all the biblical visions of the Christian
life by ourselves, but surely we are called to take them all seriously,
to ask what they mean for our lives, and to be open to what they
might call forth from us and from our communities.

Avoiding Idolatry

To fail to preserve diversity, to think of *our* point of view as the
right one or the *only* one, is, in some sense, to risk idolatry. The
biblical materials condemn an idolatry of idols made with hands.
The Bible also condemns an idolatry of idols made with words
and ideas. We are guilty of idolatry made with words when we
lift up a creed or a theology or a set of ethics as if it were absolute,
as if these human-made formulations about God were what we
trusted and could count on. When we make absolutes of these
things, we imply that we have captured God in our words or in
our beliefs or in our moral prescriptions. We have failed to distinguish God from religion, failed to distinguish the reality of God
from our human doctrines *about* God, our forms of worship, and
our moral convictions. Only as we challenge these verbal idols
and see them as our own human efforts to understand God can
we really open ourselves to put our faith not in words about God
but in the actual reality of God.

This is where the doubting and questioning function of our

faith obviously becomes so important. If we think of faith as belief in certain truth statements, then we will view doubt as incompatible with faith. On the other hand, if we think of faith as trust in the reality of God, then we will need to question our formulations of belief so that we do not put our faith in the formulations rather than in God. It has been said that there are two ways to avoid idolatry of language about God—either say nothing about God or say enough things about God so that it is clear no one thing is an absolute. Preserving the differing perspectives of the New Testament enables us to say enough things about God and God's work in Jesus that it is clear no one tradition is an absolute. We can and should embrace formulations of the faith with great conviction, but always with humility, with a dimension of tentativeness, with some aspect of uncertainty; for every perspective about God is shaped by our human limitations and circumstances, and every perspective needs to be seen in relation to other perspectives.

Stated positively, we need the diversity from the New Testament to ensure that our theology remains constructive rather than oppressive of others who would disagree, confessional rather than dogmatic, continually reminding us that while God is revealed, God is also always hidden. Being finite, we will discern only some of the revelation, and we will discern it in distorted ways. The legitimacy of other religious perspectives rooted in the New Testament rightly calls into question the adequacy of one theology, subverts our absolutes, and keeps us off balance. Such an approach keeps our Christian thinking in motion, in ferment, so that we are always forging out fresh understandings of God, of Jesus, of the church, of the human condition, and so on. Such ferment is the fertile seedbed for renewal. Thus, the diversity in the New Testament not only offers us renewal; it also helps to preserve our faith from idolatry.

Canonical Respect for Diversity

One major problem with idolatry is that it fosters intolerance. When we think we have the corner on truth and the absolutely right ethics, then others become "different" and inferior. We go beyond disagreement and advocacy for our point of view to develop an attitude of intolerant superiority toward others. At best, such an attitude of intolerance marginalizes and isolates others. At worst, we may develop a zeal to dominate and suppress the convictions of others. Under certain circumstances, we may go so far as to think we have the right to persecute or harass others. Zealous attitudes in Christianity and in other religions are the source of much conflict and suffering in our world today.

As a collection of writings, the New Testament undercuts such intolerance. Taken alone, each biblical writing may well lend itself to the kind of certainty that could be distorted into intolerance, for each New Testament writer speaks with a tone of certainty in presenting a clear-cut choice between this right way and that wrong way. Each New Testament writing tends to draw a line of judgment whereby those who have chosen the good way are on one side and those who have chosen the evil way are on the other side. However, the New Testament writings as a collection relativize the absoluteness of each individual writing, because together the writings draw the line of judgment at so many different places! As we have seen, Paul draws the line over the issue of faith in God's justification by grace, Mark over the willingness to relinquish self for the good news, Matthew over the righteous fulfilling of the Law, Luke over the merciful commitment to the poor, and John over the spiritual knowing of God. Fortunately, multiple lines of judgment lead us to be consistent with the fundamental New Testament conviction that "judgment ultimately lies with God alone." Thus, the canon leads us to shift from a limited either-or mentality to a both-and mentality in the larger embrace of God's wisdom.

So instead of fostering intolerance, the biblical canon fosters great tolerance. It fosters a commitment to see diversity as a fundamental part of the quest for truth and life. Personally, we may have a sense of certitude about the truth and reality of what we believe; that is, we may have enough assurance in our convictions to live and die for them. Yet we still never have the kind of certainty that gives us license for intolerant treatment of others. The diversity in the New Testament subverts that kind of certainty and promotes a diversity of perspectives.

Thus, canonical diversity fosters much more than tolerance; it promotes mutual interdependence. It enables us to recognize that while our own view may be faithful, it is always incomplete. It may be truthful, but it is never adequate. By itself, every perspective is limited and relative to its own time and place. Thus, various contemporary Christian communities are dependent on one another to manifest the whole biblical tradition of the good news. Each tradition has a vested interest in seeing that *other* denominational traditions and cultural expressions of Christianity remain viable and thrive! We need to encourage one another and to count on one another to do together what we cannot do alone.

Reading to Renew Our Own Traditions

Studying the diversity in the New Testament may give us an opportunity to recover the roots of our own cultural or denominational tradition. The variety of New Testament visions places our own tradition in sharper relief and enables us to look in new ways at the distinct theology, ethics, and practices of our own tradition. Thus, one step toward renewal might be to identify the writings within the canon that have been formative for our own community and to study them again. Such a recovery of the roots of our own tradition can enliven the gospel message so close to us and infuse it anew with the Spirit. We may discern how we have domesticated our biblical tradition or interpreted it to support our own lifestyle or blunted the challenge to our comfortable existence or ignored aspects of the model that would lead to transformation. Also, by returning to the origins of our own tradition, perhaps we can identify what it neglects.

If one of the vocational purposes of a church or a denomination is to bear faithfully its own distinct tradition on behalf of the whole church, it is important to have renewal from one's biblical roots. In addition, an awareness of biblical diversity enables us to compare and contrast our own particular biblical traditions with those of others and thereby to see more clearly the distinctive contribution that our community of faith makes to the larger stream of contemporary Christianity. However, by itself, renewing our own biblical traditions is not fully adequate. It is not enough simply to have isolated communities renewing their own traditions and each doing its own thing. If diversity is a distinguishing mark of authentic Christian life, then each community will want to find ways also to incorporate biblical diversity into its own life and to have meaningful interactions with communities bearing different traditions.

Renewal from Another Biblical Model

We can read for renewal by studying in-depth one biblical tradition other than our own, thereby broadening our experience of what it means to be Christian. We can study another biblical model for the purpose of being transformed, renewed, and shaped by it in personal and community life. For example, a parish or prayer group might attempt to "think Markan" or to ask what it means to be "Johannine Christians" in our time. Parishioners might view their daily life, current events, and popular culture through the eyes of Matthew or Luke. Participants could ask: In our situation, what biblical model will best challenge and renew us? Just what might that model mean for twenty-first century Christian life in our particular time and place? How does this model address the context of our community in new and challenging ways? The idea is not to remake totally the community on the model of a given biblical writing, but to see how the dynamic of a different biblical writing might shape a parish anew.

We may need time to live with a fresh model long enough to know it well, to see its full implications, to pursue our questions and concerns, so that we really hear the good news, are changed by it, do not soften its offense, do not lose the experience of otherness in such a way that we end up funneling the rich diversity into the narrow compass of our own experience or tradition. A famous preacher once began a sermon on "the born-again experience" by declaring, "It is sometimes proper to declare what one does not know," in effect saying, "I am going to preach to you today on something I myself have not experienced, but I will be faithful to the text." Would that we as Christians had such courage to be faithful to the otherness of the text in such a way that we proclaimed what we ourselves had not necessarily experienced, proclaimed what we ourselves find difficult, struggled with what makes us uneasy or uncomfortable, grappled with what leads us to repent, opened ourselves to what expands our views of God and the world—and shared our own struggles and resistance in the proclaiming.

Renewal through Encountering Many Models

A community could study not just one other biblical model but many models from the New Testament. Such a process would explore a range of ways to be Christian. Such a study of diversity in the New Testament might help us get in touch with the diversity already there in our own parish communities. For example, after studying the biblical models treated in this book, different people might identify which biblical writing is their favorite and why it is their favorite. If differing voices in a parish find their own views reflected in the Bible, this may give them courage to be more assertive about expressing their points of view. It may provide an opportunity to discover why people are drawn to different visions of the Christian life and how members might mutually enrich each other by these differences.

Thus, exploring the diversity in the New Testament might well renew Christian communities by fostering an appreciation for diversity in and of itself. Many Christian communities are comprised of people who are pretty much alike from a cultural point of view—same race, ethnic group, economic class, and nationality. By being in parishes composed of people who are alike, we miss the exhilaration of being united in the Spirit with people different from ourselves. We lose the possibility of mutual enrichment and interactive support that diverse people in God's creation were meant to provide each other. However, many parishes are quite diverse—composed of people from different denominational backgrounds, having moved from other parts of the country, from different ethnic or racial or national backgrounds, or located in changing neighborhoods. An appreciation for the diversity in the New Testament may help us to see our own diversity in the positive light of the gospel and lead us to foster even greater diversity in the composition of our communities.

An appreciation for diversity may lead us to hunger for a Christian community that encompasses greater diversity and to be intentional about creating such a community. However, we need to be careful. The purpose of embracing diversity in parishes is not somehow to make our communities a little more colorful but to experience genuine renewal from others. Therefore, when we are seeking to reflect the universality of the gospel, it may not be enough to be in favor of diversity; we may need also to be against exclusivity, against discrimination. We may need to identify and change the things about our community that prevent people of differing social locations from participating. In this way we can actively work to counter the forces that would inhibit diversity and at the same time we can actively work to create communities that embrace difference.

A genuine celebration of diversity could enable communities to lift up the various cultural and ethnic expressions of Christianity and to ask how all these traditions could be incorporated so as to enrich their life together. A celebration of diversity may help people clarify their own beliefs and commitments in a safe environment where people are respectful of one another. In fact, an appreciation for religious differences might well lead to a greater appreciation for all differences among people—gender, origins, race, ethnic traditions, socioeconomic location, regional roots, training, education, and personal experiences. A commitment to diversity implies that we ought intentionally to seek out people who are different from us and work to understand them, learn from them, and respect them in their differences.

But let us not assume that sharing differences will be easy. We are often afraid to talk with each other about our differences for fear of conflict or for fear of being marginalized or for fear of threatening someone's faith. Yet when people do begin to talk, they are often amazed at the different points of view members have about the Bible and in their convictions. Unfortunately, by itself, dialogue does not always assure mutual understanding. Unless it is motivated by a spiritual appreciation for the value of diversity, dialogue may only expose the depths of our intolerance rather than create a bridge of respect. Experiencing the full range of diversity requires respect and the genuine interest in others and in the cultures of others. The process of sharing should provide an opportunity to give voice to everyone and to learn to listen well.

Here there can be no assumption that one's own views are superior, no denigrating or dismissing the views of others, but an eagerness to understand, to learn, and to grow. It is more important to listen actively than to argue, more important to understand empathetically than to correct or contradict. The main task is for each person to explain his or her own views in a safe context, and in turn to listen *carefully* to the views of others. Participants can clarify their views and explain why they may agree and differ with each other. Dialogue does not mean we avoid affirming our convictions, but that we in no way impose them on others. People need to be honored for expressing their views, for struggling with them, and for being open to learn and grow from the views of others. Certain guidelines for discussion may be helpful, assuring that people will not dominate or interrupt but will listen for understanding and ask for clarification, and together hear the experiences, the biblical traditions, and the personal stories that have shaped our differing views.

Renewal through Relationships with Congregations of Other Traditions

Diversity in Christianity is honored when we recognize that different denominations are legitimately rooted in the different New Testament witnesses (including many independent congregations not affiliated with a denomination). For example, discussions between Roman Catholics and Lutherans suggest that while the Lutheran view is faithful to Paul's theology, the Roman Catholic view is faithful to Matthew's view. Now what does it say about fellowship between denominations when both groups—though in disagreement—are equally and validly rooted in the biblical materials? We could engage in Bible study with a parish from another denomination and perhaps choose to study a writing that is important to that other community. Studying the Bible with other Christian groups should not lead to assimilation or uniformity or conformity but rather should be based on mutual respect and cooperation.

The choice of a partner for a common Bible study would be enhanced by cultural, racial, ethnic, or economic differences. In light of the focus of this book, key questions to explore might be: What New Testament traditions does your church or ethnic group draw from for faith and life? What is your "canon within the canon"? What traditions does your group tend to avoid or neglect? How might cooperation between these two particular communities complement or mutually enhance the ministry of each other?

Such shared Bible study might lead to yoking or covenanting between communities or parishes—for community worship services, to address neighborhood problems, or to strengthen common ministries. Cooperation can be energizing and can serve to revitalize faith. Yet cooperate efforts in a common program or task may not be easy. An experience of mutuality across traditions is often hard won, because everyone is sure their distinctiveness is more central than others, and no one wants to sacrifice their distinctiveness in the process of cooperation. We may find ourselves treating differences in terms of what is superior and inferior and then developing hierarchical structures of cooperation that lead to domination and control. Instead, what we need is to treat differences in terms of partnerships and develop structures of mutuality where we can share leadership and learn from each other.

Genuinely mutual relationships between parishes are especially difficult to achieve when one group comes from the "dominant" culture and the other from an oppressed or marginalized community. Nevertheless, such opportunities may enable us to deal with the oppressions and victimizations that have occurred between different Christian denominations, racial groups, and social classes. Unless we use these opportunities to overcome oppression, diversity will only be a superficial pastime of comfortable people without the social transformation we need for either the church or the society. Seeing the common rootage of different churches in different biblical traditions may help to enhance mutual respect.

Thus, the commitment to diversity may involve deep soul-searching. There have often been long-standing relationships of hostility between denominational and between cultural traditions. In a moving worship service in Bolivia years ago, I witnessed representatives of several Christian traditions confess their sins and the sins of their traditions against each other and then ask God "to be forgiven as we forgive those who have sinned against us." We are all called to a deep renunciation of discrimination, of stereotyping, of religious arrogance, of ethnocentrism, of racism, and of the lack of full respect. Such renunciation may require on the part of some a recognition of responsibility and a profound repentance, and it may require on the part of others a commitment to forgiveness and openness despite hurt and ambivalence. We can learn from the early Christians how they dealt with and celebrated their new-found diversity—through love, forgiveness, relinquishment, reconciliation, shared joy, and the acceptance of justification for all. Relationships between people are often complex and confusing, but what meaningful revelry in the Spirit can come when we have learned to honor our differences in a deeper unity of the Christian walk!

Creating New Models

There is yet another challenge from New Testament diversity. Why not make an original contribution to the diversity in the shape of parish life? Why not imitate the creativity of the early church and follow the Spirit in our own reinvention of Christian communities for our time? We have said that the early church represented an explosion of creative experiments in lifestyle, ethical behavior, community order, and religious rituals. It was this explosion of Christianity taking place in so many different cultural contexts throughout the Mediterranean world that explains the diversity we have in the New Testament. Each writer forged the traditions into new configurations that addressed particular communities, baptizing familiar metaphors and experiences as means to live the good news about Jesus.

This, then, is another way to be faithful to the New Testament, not just to imitate in our time one biblical tradition or another, but to imitate the creativity of the New Testament writers. Faithfulness to the New Testament calls us to be creative as the first Christians were creative, to transform our traditions in order to address the particular context in which our communities are located—as the writers of the New Testament did for their communities. If we learn anything from the New Testament, it is that the work of God is always creative *and* radically contextual. The diversity of the New Testament reveals that God works in particular, concrete situations to address people where they are and to bring the kingdom into their midst.

Why not seek to create a fresh contextual expression of Christianity in parish life for your own time and place? After all, the whole history of theology is a history of such innovation and creativity. Why not apply that creativity to the Christian life of a local congregation? Out of the raw materials of their geographical locale, urban or rural setting, cultural backgrounds, ethnic make-up, natural resources, regional context, the needs and struggles of the people, and the shared context of American culture, parishes might create fresh expressions of the Christian life and mission in local situations. In such an imitation of biblical creativity, a parish community could seek to be faithful to its biblical and ecclesial traditions and still provide contemporary expressions of the faith.

Commitment to Diversity within Denominational Structures

Denominations often strive for uniformity in theological reflection, congregational organization, worship patterns, educational materials, and mission emphases, while the actual needs of specific congregations vary greatly depending on social location—racial and ethnic composition, social class, educational level, and regional context. A generic model for parish life does not meet all of these contextual situations. Parishes need to be flexible and adaptable—when the parish is responding to its context or when there is need for renewal or when times change or when neighborhoods undergo transition or when the makeup of the parish changes or when people need a new challenge. Biblical diversity implies that at different times and places, denominational life could manifest itself in Mark's model of courage in the face of risk or Luke's model of confronting the oppression in our society or the model of John's deeply spiritual experience of community or a fresh expression of the Christian life. Hence, each denomination has a responsibility to find ways to embrace biblical diversity.

In some sense, of course, diversity is built into every denomination, for every denomination has a history of responding to many parts of the Bible. Actually, there is undoubtedly greater diversity already available within the history and life of each denomination than most people realize.

However, when a denomination relies too much on one biblical model, there is a tendency to emphasize it to the point that a vital balance is lost, and a great strength becomes a liability. Again, let me give a hypothetical illustration from my own Lutheran tradition, rooted in Pauline thought. According to the Pauline model, reconciliation is the primary model for dealing with conflict at the congregational level. However, we may have a circumstance that calls for a different model. For example, there may be injustice or economic exploitation in the city in which the congregation is located and there is a need to operate out of the prophetic model evident in the Gospel of Luke. This model lends itself to confronting the inequities in the society, the oppression of the many by a few, and the absence of justice and mercy in the corridors of power. Such a prophetic ministry may test the unity of the church. When the only model of parish life is the Pauline model of "reconciliation," then conflict and confrontation for the gospel might be seen as incompatible with parish life. It is difficult, for example, to be a parish leader on Paul's model and carry on a prophetic ministry on Luke's model.

There are liabilities any time a denomination limits itself to only one biblical model. Those who follow the Pauline model may emphasize justification to the exclusion of sanctification or they may focus on grace to the neglect of actions to transform the social order. By itself, Mark's model may lead to a glorification of suffering. By itself, Matthew's model may end up as a new legalism. Luke's prophetic model can be empty if it is carried out without its vital rootedness in the Holy Spirit. Without the whole canon, John's model of spirituality can lead to exclusiveness or to the neglect of the poor and oppressed.

The key question is, How can a denomination preserve its identity and still encompass diversity? There are no easy answers to this dilemma. Clearly, each tradition needs to see its vocation in light of its formative traditions. Being rooted securely in these traditions and exercising the flexibility in these primary traditions is often the first step in openness to diversity. When the church knows its identity well, it can incorporate other biblical models and other ways of being Christian into its life. Again, adaptability provided by the diversity of biblical models does not make Presbyterians into non-Presbyterians or Methodists into non-Methodists or Roman Catholics into something else. Nor need such flexibility threaten the basic identities of our communities. If we see that the primary mission of each denomination is to preserve the model of their particular tradition for the whole church, then we can also enrich our tradition by the experience of living out of other biblical traditions as well. Even though the struggle is difficult, such a struggle is a crucial way in which we are called to be faithful to the whole Bible in our time.

Diversity in the World

The church exists for the sake of the world. Therefore, our commitment to diversity in our communities is but a prelude to our commitment to diversity among all the people God has created. We began by saying that diversity was integral to God's creation of life and an indispensable factor in human survival. If we learned the early Christian ways of embracing diversity, our churches might be able to help our culture deal with the explosion of diversity that we are presently experiencing in our world. We live now in an era in which very few parts of the world are isolated from pluralism. We live in a world that is a global village, and every village is somewhat global. Given the foundational diversity inherent in Christianity, Christians can be at the forefront of embracing diversity and growing from it. Our communities can become models for the society in terms of how to communicate cross-culturally, how to work through divisive differences, how to foster genuine mutuality, how to affirm a commitment to other people amidst diversity. Such paradigms for living can provide alternatives to the strategies of separation and antagonism that characterize so much of the society.

In some ways, our society may already be ahead of the church. There are courses and conferences everywhere showing teachers how to foster multiculturality in the classroom. There are workshops and training sessions for people in business to learn how to appreciate and to work mutually with those of other cultures and languages. As Christians, we can learn from these efforts. However, we can also be active leaders and participants in this process. We have much to contribute. For we have learned at the deepest levels the value God places on the varieties of people, we have experienced God's commitment to justice and to reconciliation, and we embrace the call to mutual interdependence as the way to enhance human life.

It is central to our mission in the world that Christians be catalysts for creative fostering of an appreciation for diversity in our roles as teachers, factory workers, barbers, physicians, government employees, office managers, and so on. We can be agents of God who have learned from our Christian experience how to renounce intolerance, how to value people different from ourselves, how to live out of a vision for God's creation that cherishes all. We can resist the tendency for groups in the face of differences to hunker down, to become isolated, to engage in stereotyping and scapegoating, to separate and wall off those who are different, and to consider all that is strange as deviant. The church of many cultures can provide agents of reconciliation who seek to bring all together into the dawn of the kingdom. Because the church exists not for itself but for the world, this is central to our mission.

Summary

We are living at a time when each denomination is struggling to remain faithful to its identity and at the same time be open to the pluralism of our society. Renewal from the diversity in the New Testament can contribute in positive ways to this struggle. For it is a reminder that there is not just one way to believe, not just one way to live as a Christian, not just one way to be religious, not just one way to be human. Renewal from the New Testament places a legitimacy upon pluralism and variety. Renewal from the diversity in the New Testament puts us in touch with the roots of the diversity of all creation and encourages us to honor one another. It shows us how we can learn from one another so that our lives are enriched and deepened. Through such renewal we may capture a fresh excitement about being Christian and a new understanding of our purposes as human beings in the world at this time and place in history.

Further Reading

Barr, David. *New Testament Story: An Introduction.* New York: Wadsworth, 1995.

Boff, Leonardo. *Ecclesiogenesis: The Base Communities Reinvent the Church.* Maryknoll: Orbis, 1986.

Brennan, Patrick. *Re-Imagining the Parish: Base Communities, Adulthood, and Family Consciousness.* New York: Crossroad, 1990.

Coalter, Milton et al., editors. *The Diversity of Discipleship: The Presbyterians and Twentieth Century Christian Witness.* Louisville: Westminster/ John Knox, 1991.

Conger, Y. *Diversity and Communion.* Mystic, Conn.: Twenty-Third Publications, 1984.

Costas, Orlando, editor. *One Faith Many Cultures.* Maryknoll: Orbis, 1988.

Craig, Robert and Robert Worley. *Dry Bones Live: Helping Congregations Discover New Life*. Louisville: Westminster/ John Knox, 1992.

DeYoung, Curtiss Paul. *Coming Together: The Bible's Message in an Age of Diversity*. Valley Forge: Judson Press, 1995.

Fitzpatrick, Joseph. *One Church Many Cultures: The Challenge of Diversity*. Kansas City: Sheed and Ward, 1987.

Gittins, Anthony. *Gifts and Strangers: Meeting the Challenge of Inculturation*. New York: Paulist, 1989.

Guthrie, S. *Diversity in Faith, Unity in Christ*. Philadelphia: Westminster, 1986.

Jewett, Robert. *The Captain America Complex: The Dilemma of Zealous Nationalism*. Santa Fe: Bear & Company, 1984.

_____. *Paul the Apostle to America: Cultural Trends and Pauline Scholarship*. Louisville: Westminster/ John Knox, 1994.

Kim, Young-Il, editor. *Knowledge, Attitude, and Experience: Ministry in the Cross-Cultural Context*. Nashville: Abingdon, 1992.

Lee, Jung Young. *Marginality: The Key to Multicultural Theology*. Minneapolis: Fortress Press, 1995.

Mead, Loren. *The Once and Future Church: Reinventing the Congregation for a New Mission Frontier*. Washington, D.C.: Alban Institute, 1991.

Palmer, Parker. *The Company of Strangers: Christians and the Renewal of America's Public Life*. New York: Crossroad, 1981.

Rhoads, David. "The New Testament: An Introduction" (video course available from SELECT, Trinity Lutheran Seminary, Columbus, Ohio.

Russell, Keith. *In Search of the Church: New Testament Images for Tomorrow's Congregations*. New York: Alban Institute, 1994.

Russell, Letty. *The Future of Partnership*. Philadelphia: Westminster, 1979.

_____. *Growth in Partnership*. Philadelphia: Westminster, 1981.

Schaller, Lyle. *Create Your Own Future: Alternatives for Long-Range Planning Committees*. Nashville: Abingdon, 1991.

_____. *Innovations in Ministry: Models for the 21st Century*. Nashville: Abingdon, 1994.

Schreiter, Robert. *Constructing Local Theologies*. Maryknoll: Orbis, 1992.

Thistlethwaite, Susan. *Metaphors for the Contemporary Church*. New York: Pilgrim Press, 1983.

Thistlethwaite, Susan and Mary Potter Engel, editors. *Lift Every Voice: Constructing Christian Theologies from the Underside*. New York: Harper and Row, 1990.

Epilogue
Reflections on Unity

ACKNOWLEDGING DIVERSITY IN THE NEW TESTAMENT and encouraging diversity in Christianity may be threatening ideas, because they raise in us the fear that there will be no unity or coherence or community. We have a longing for unity, a deep desire to find the things that connect us and bind us across differences—even, and perhaps especially, in the midst of conflict. Indeed, diversity without some form of unity will end up in chaos. Differences that are not related to each other in some way—whether by complementarity or paradox or tension or even contradiction—may be destructive.

Unity and diversity are not polar opposites. Rather, they belong together in a complementary relationship with each other. The question is: How can we talk about unity without compromising diversity? Here we will reflect briefly on some of the ways we seek unity in the face of diversity and then ask what it is that does ultimately unify us as Christians.

Unity by Agreement

Often we have taken the approach that unity is based on what people can agree on. As a congregation or denomination or groups of denominations, we work toward a statement of beliefs or practices or convictions to which different individuals or groups are able to give common assent. This approach to unity leads to greater understanding, cooperation, and integration within or between groups, sometimes even to organizational merger. Furthermore, there can be a great sense of solidarity among people who have agreed upon the same values, convictions, and common responses to the good news. It is good and positive to work for unity through agreement.

In fact, it is by means of such unity by agreement that we have diverse denominational identities and diverse ethnic identities within denominations in the first place. As we have noted, the concern to foster diversity is not an argument against distinct denominational identities. It is crucial to have different denominational and ethnic identities in the Christian faith, and to recognize at the same time that such identities represent a smaller circle of unity. Beyond that is the broader circle of unity we share with other denominations and with the church as a whole. The idea of diversity is not that we all become so diverse that there are no longer differences among us. Then we would lose our identities and, paradoxically, our diversity as well. Thus, unity by agreement among discrete groups within Christianity becomes an important way we preserve diversity.

Treating agreement as the basis for unity, however, brings with it certain perils. For example, when we focus on those things upon which we can agree, we may ignore or disallow our differences and fail to honor diversity itself as a constitutive dimension of community. Also, unity based on agreement may end up being narrowly circumscribed. The statements we can agree on probably would not be encompassing enough to embrace most viewpoints in the New Testament! The result is that individuals or groups that are rooted in other parts of the New Testament become excluded and marginalized. Statements of agreement become norms for inclusion or exclusion or they define a center in relation to which others are considered to be either near the middle or on the periphery.

The result may be that a drive toward unity as agreement becomes, in practice, hegemony—one group dominating or silencing other groups outside or inside the community. This dynamic explains why marginal groups, oppressed peoples, and minority voices are often wary of talk about unity, because the drive for unity may tend to eliminate or diminish or assimilate their distinctiveness. Unity that is based on rigid demands for agreement can end up fragmenting community internally and externally, and at worst it results in oppression. As one person put it: "If we all had to agree on what it means to be Christian, we would never be united."

Unity Based on Commonalities

Another way of working toward unity is to identify commonalities. A mutual discovery of commonalities between different groups will be less likely to lead to a misuse of power. When we focus on commonalities rather than agreement, we talk about the things that already bind us. We identify in a general sense what the groups share in common, without setting norms for inclusion or exclusion. An appreciation for the diversity in the New Testament ensures that commonalities will be defined on grounds broad enough to guarantee respect for diversity.

Commonalities function at a deeper and broader level than statements of agreement. The distinction between unity as agreement and the identification of commonalities can be illustrated by the following example. An interdenominational/multiethnic committee was responsible for a service of praise for the neighborhood at Thanksgiving. The committee wanted to provide a service in which everyone felt included. They thought about listing a number of hymns and then polling the various denominational and ethnic groups to see what songs everyone could agree on. However, they realized this attempt to find agreement would result in conflicts and reduce the offerings to common denominators. So the committee looked at a deeper level for the commonalities shared by the different groups. They realized that everyone shared in common the desire to praise God. So, they asked the various participating groups to suggest what songs each community found most expressive in *their* praise of God. The result was a wonderful celebration in which everyone felt they had a stake without dominating any other group. And everyone benefited from experiencing the ways *other people* praised God.

We find our foundational commonalities among the differing New Testament views—worship of God, allegiance to Jesus, the conviction of his resurrection, a celebration of love, the desire to praise, renewal in the Holy Spirit, an openness to others, and so on. Efforts among differing groups to find shared commonalities keeps us rooted in what is fundamental to us as Christians. In turn, embracing each other in these commonalities can provide a ballast for us to deal with significant differences between us.

Unity through Appreciation of Differences

We can find unity through our common commitment to diversity itself. If we see diversity as a positive good, then we begin to seek ways in which differences can be understood, honored, and mutually enriching. By having the courage to deal "up front" with differences, we establish the constitutive importance of diversity for human community. By stressing differences, we make certain that the unity is not narrowly defined. In a sense, such "enrichment through differences" parallels the biblical canon, where different visions exist side by side in one scripture.

A commitment to diversity will begin with a mutual desire to understand differences and to accept one another with those differences. At minimum, this can simply mean to "agree to disagree." However, it can be much more than that. We can honor our differences, continue the discussion, and discover what we can learn from each other. For example, in discussions between such diverse groups as the Presbyterian and Greek Orthodox Churches, participants might conclude that they would ruin a good thing if they tried to work toward unity or union between these two communions. Each group bears very different biblical traditions and each group contributes to Christian life and mission in significantly different ways. So, instead of seeking unity by agreement, they might be reconciled to each other not in spite of but because of their differences. In this way, the communities can embrace their relationship as complementary and mutually enriching.

Unity as Participation

The longing for unity across differences can sometimes be met by the common willingness to be in the struggle together and to work toward a common life and mission together. Regardless of where we may find ourselves or others, we can appreciate the shared commitments of each and all to be faithful in a variety of ways to the biblical materials as we participate with each other in the journey to follow Jesus and to have our lives shaped by the biblical witnesses to him. As such, we can participate together as partners in shared ministries and tasks that work toward a common vision. Such an experience represents "unity as cooperation." In this case, differing groups with differing gifts produce a synergy of activity by which groups reinforce and complement each other without in any way compromising their diversity.

Participation enables us to speak of community rather than unity, of interrelatedness rather than uniformity, of togetherness rather than oneness. Thus, we may find a ballast for the differences not in what we agree upon, but in the experience of participating together in a process or in a common task. When this occurs, we discover that we need the differences to help us work better together in life and mission.

Unity through a Vision of Inclusion

The New Testament writings express numerous visions of inclusive unity—all meant to embrace greater diversity than what the writers' previous experiences of unity had embraced. For example, in the Gospels Jesus is recorded as the one who broke down boundaries between those included and those excluded—unclean, Gentiles, sinners, tax collectors. Paul includes Gentiles in his vision of a time when "Every knee shall bow and every tongue confess that Jesus Christ is Lord." The author of Ephesians celebrates God's act in Jesus, which creates out of Jews and Gentiles "one new humanity." Luke cites the prophecy that "All flesh will behold the salvation of God" and describes the Christian mission to "the ends of the earth." The author of Revelation depicts the worship of God by people from "every tribe, tongue, nation, and people" uniting in one glorious hymn to God and to the lamb.

Each of these writers sought to embrace great diversity in a broad vision of unity. Each of these visions of unity is predicated on allegiance to Jesus as the great unifying force that holds diversity together. Such a commitment to inclusivity provides the impetus to keep pushing out the boundaries of unity to include greater and greater diversity. In faithfulness to these visions, we can strive to encompass many diverse people in the widest expression of God's love.

The Canon as Model

The canon can be a model not only for the diversity of the church but also for the unity of the church. Here we have many diverse viewpoints as well as many different visions of unity held together by their inclusion in the canon.

The canon also helps us to define the limits of diversity. While much was included in the canon, there was also much that was left out. Using the canon as a measure of diversity makes it clear that not anything goes. We must struggle with crucial issues surrounding the legitimate outer limits of what it means to be faithful Christians. For example, those who would deny the humanity of Jesus or reject the God of Israel as the God of Jesus Christ would not find their roots in the canon. Also, groups functioning under a Christian banner that actively promote hatred, greed, exploitation, oppression, violence, or prejudice would not easily come under the umbrella of the New Testament canon.

However, using the canon to identify parameters of Christian diversity does have certain difficulties. Many Christian groups would want to extend Christian authority beyond the canon. For example, the Roman Catholic church also gives great weight to the tradition of the church as authoritative. Many Protestant groups give weight to their foundational documents either as witnesses added to scripture or as the basis for the interpretation of scripture. Lutherans affirm allegiance to the Book of Concord, Presbyterians to the Westminster Confession. Some groups have wanted to add modern writings to the canon, such as Martin Luther King's "Letter from a Birmingham Jail."

On the other hand, using the biblical canon to express the parameters of Christian diversity might be problematic from the opposite direction. There are parts of the canon itself that many people do not treat as authoritative for their life and worship. Most do this by ignoring certain biblical traditions, such as the admonition to wash one another's feet, the invitation to give up wealth to the poor, or the command to love one's enemy. Moreover, some people reject outright those parts of scripture that lend themselves to intolerance or oppression, such as the sayings that support slavery or the ethical codes that foster a patriarchal treatment of women or passages expressing anti-semitism or an attitude of zealous hatred toward opponents of Christianity as antichrists.

Thus, even seeing the biblical canon as a model for the diversity of the church is not without difficulties. It is very difficult for Christian groups who repudiate certain assumptions and practices supported by certain writings in the Bible to accept other Christian groups who embrace them. The converse is also true. It is difficult for groups who accept certain assumptions and practices (for example, the view of the Pastoral letters that women should be subordinate to men) to accept other groups who do not. While it is helpful to see the Bible as a model for diversity in the church, there are problems with identifying it as the basis for the acceptable extent and limit of diversity. Thus, the canon cannot serve as the ultimate basis for unity.

Unity Given by God

In the final analysis, human beings are united by virtue of being an integral part of God's creation. Thus, despite our human efforts to differentiate ourselves from others in some fundamental way or to make ourselves believe we are not really like certain other people, there is a common sharing of humanity that is incontrovertible. Sometimes by God's grace, people have existential or spiritual experiences of this unifying ground of reality that enables them to know they are part of the seamless web of life. They may not understand the mystery of how all of life is so interconnected or be able to explain their experience to others. Nevertheless, such experiences become the basis out of which people can relish in new ways the unity as well as the incredible diversity of creation.

Ultimately, religion is not what unites us. Religion is not God, but our human responses to God. All our ideas of unity are human constructs. Thus neither our doctrines nor our ethics nor our rituals nor our piety nor our customs, neither our commonalities nor our agreements are, in the end, an adequate basis for unity. The *reality of God* is the basis for our unity—"One God ... who is above all and in all and through all" (Ephesians 4:5). We have many gifts but one lord, many services but one God, many activities but one God. Thus a "theology of unity" might conclude that unity is a reality of life given to us in the life of God, a given to be accepted and achieved, a given to be received and yet still hoped for.

Redemption in Christ also offers unity as a given. In the Pauline model, God has already acted to reconcile all people to God's self in Jesus' death on the cross, which removed all barriers to reconciliation between human beings. Therefore, Paul understands that Christians are ambassadors of this reconciliation, announcing justification to people as an accomplished fact and inviting them to embrace it as a way of life. This givenness of the experience of redemption enabled Paul to accept the particularity of each cultural and ethnic group he encountered because he was not placing human standards as prerequisites. Rather, he saw all people through the eyes of faith, as people for whom Christ had already died.

Again, people often know the peace of the Holy Spirit that enables them to experience reconciliation with others at a root level, which in turn empowers them to accept and honor diversity as fundamental—"making every effort to maintain the unity of the Spirit in the bond of peace" (Ephesians 4:3).

Such unity lies in the mystery of God. In one sense, it is already achieved by virtue of our participation in the ongoing process of creation. On the other hand, unity is obviously not yet achieved. We await it and hope for it and work for it as agents of God in creation. When we understand that unity is God-given, then our efforts to come to agreement, to relish our commonalities, to become inclusive, to appreciate differences, to participate together in a process, can be seen as our human efforts to celebrate and to achieve the unity God provides.

Thus, in the end, the basis for our unity is not provided by what various groups agree to do or to believe. Unity is provided in and by the participation of God with us, for the Spirit of God unifies us at a level beyond words and actions, at a level too deep for words and actions, as we express our own longing to be part of God's people and to do God's work. And the Spirit moves us ever outward toward human solidarity with all God's creatures. The unity that is given is the unity that all humans are part of God's ongoing creation: Christian or Muslim or Hindu or atheist or humanist. All people are united by being creatures of God who are inextricably woven into the intricate fabric of all creation. God is active everywhere in the world, not simply among Christians, as God continues moment by moment to create and sustain our human lives and the world in which we live. Even when we do not respond to God's call, even when we are sinful and hostile to God, even amidst our most extreme differences, God is present sustaining the world and longing with us for its fulfillment.

Even broader than humanity, there is the unity that encompasses the diversity of all creation. As Paul wrote, "For the creation waits with eager longing for the revealing of the children of God" (Romans 8:19). And the book of Revelation envisions that a time is coming, indeed now is, when "every creature in heaven and on earth and under the earth and in the sea" (5:13) will give to the living God blessing and honor and glory. Knowing and living out of this unity, even now, is an adequate human vocation for our time.

Study Guide for
The Challenge of Diversity

Some Suggestions for Parish Life

1. An adult education group might spend several weeks studying the different writings in the New Testament, perhaps in conjunction with the chapters in this book. The class might be held with another church or several churches, perhaps of different backgrounds.

2. Engage the whole parish in a study of one biblical book over a period of time. Consider a comprehensive approach with small groups, Bible studies, sermons, sermon dialogues, church school programs for all ages, learning and telling biblical stories, private and family devotions, library offerings, book groups, and listening to tapes of the New Testament writings.

3. The three-year lectionary of many churches focuses successively on each of the first three Gospels: in the first year Matthew, in the second year Mark, and in the third year Luke. Lessons from John are dispersed in clusters throughout the three years. A congregation could spend a whole year studying each of the Gospels. A series of sermons coupled with classes could feature that biblical writing.

4. The lectionary has series of lessons that are devoted to specific Old Testament writings, to different letters of Paul, as well as to the Catholic Epistles, the Acts of the Apostles, and the book of Revelation. Study these writings during the weeks they appear in the lectionary or during a sermon series on a biblical writing. Form a group to assist the preacher in discussing the texts beforehand and responding to the sermon afterward.

5. A group of people within the parish could study Luke (for example) and covenant together to seek to live the Lukan vision for the Christian life.

6. A congregation might identify one biblical writing as its own primary model of identity for its Christian life, incorporating the goals and visions of that gospel into the goals and programs for the parish. What would worship, church organization, mission,

162

education, and pastoral care look like from the point of view of this model? How does the study of this biblical writing stimulate growth and renewal in the parish?

7. Form "listening groups" in the congregation simply for the purpose of sharing with each other and appreciating differences in faith and life experience.

8. Assess the diversity in your congregation in terms of the many factors of different social locations and seek ways to reflect and honor that diversity in worship, study, and other aspects of life together. Formulate ways you might work intentionally to make your parish appealing and welcome to a greater diversity of people. Discuss ways in which people in your parish who are very different from each other might support and complement each other as Christians.

9. Create a new model for the life and ministry of the parish. Interpret your context, identify the human problems people are dealing with, and formulate a creative expression of the gospel in word, ritual, and organization to address your situation. Make use of the raw materials of your context to forge this fresh expression of the Christian faith.

10. Yoke with one or more congregations different from your own for the purpose of mutual understanding. Try a Bible study together using principles of respect for diversity. If there has been a history of hostility and/or oppression between these Christian groups, seek mutual reconciliation.

11. Visit different churches in your community and discuss ways in which you are different from and yet united with them.

12. With other churches from different denominations and social locations, plan a community worship service for Christian unity. Use the process for planning hymns, prayers, scripture passages, and other elements of worship as means to understand better how together we complement each other in bearing the full biblical witness to the world.

13. Form a coalition of churches to address neighborhood problems such as crime, poverty, education, and youth concerns. Use the opportunity of organizing at the grassroots level to appreciate how the ministries of the various Christian traditions are rooted in, inspired by, and shaped by the different traditions of the Bible.

Course Outline

Session 1

Preparation: Read the introduction and chapter 1.

1. Convener:* Review briefly the purpose of the book and your reasons for studying it.

2. Group:** Share your responses to the introduction to this book. Choose questions for discussion from the relevant section below.

3. Convener: Review briefly (a) the diversity in the New Testament, (b) the three ways we tend to eclipse the diversity in the New Testament, and (c) the suggestions for reading for diversity.

4. Group: Discuss chapter 1. Choose questions from the list for discussion.

5. Review the assigned preparation for the next class.

Sessions 2–6

Preparation: Read the relevant biblical writing*** and the chapter correlated with it.

1. Group: Share with each other your responses to reading the biblical writing.

2. Convener: Summarize briefly the key points of the chapter: the two ways, the human condition, the vision for life, and the means of transformation.

3. Group: Discuss the chapter. Choose questions from the relevant list for discussion.

4. Group: Compare and contrast each writing with the previous one(s) you studied.

5. Review the assigned preparation for the following week.

Session 7

Preparation: Read chapter 7 and the epilogue.

1. Group: Share your overall reactions to the book and to the five biblical writings.

2. Convener: Summarize briefly a few of the reflections on diversity from chapter 7.

3. Group: Discuss the implications of diversity for your parish. Choose questions for discussion.

4. Convener: Review briefly the key points of the epilogue.

5. Group: Discuss the epilogue. Choose questions for discussion.

6. Group: Where might your parish go from here?

* One person can carry out the role of convener or the role can be rotated from week to week. The convener may want to assign times for the various activities in relation to the overall length of the session.

** Depending on the size of the group, you may want to do the "group" activities in small groups of twos or threes. This procedure enables everyone to participate actively.

***It is best to read the relevant biblical writing in its entirety at one sitting. Where feasible, read each biblical writing aloud (in a group?) or listen to a tape of the writing. In ancient times, most Christians experienced these writings by hearing them. Seeking to recover this oral experience enhances our capacity to experience the biblical writings afresh. See the preface for information on audio and video tapes of selections from these writings.

Questions for Discussion

Introduction: Diversity

1. *As you embark on the study of diversity in the New Testament, what do you expect to find?* How do you think it might be a source of renewal? What might be the obstacles or problems? What are your fears and concerns?

2. *What Christian relationships do you have with people of other denominations?* How have these relationships enhanced your understanding of the Christian life? Does your parish include people with differing Christian backgrounds?

3. *What are the diverse ethnic backgrounds of members of your parish?* How have your ethnic backgrounds shaped your Christian experience? What are other factors of difference in social location among members? In what ways might your community become more diverse?

4. *In what ways have you experienced ethnic, cultural, religious, and political diversity in our society—work, education, neighborhood, nation, other?* What has been helpful about these relationships? What has been difficult? What resources have been available for people to deal with multiculturality? How might you deal differently with those relationships in light of this study?

Chapter 1: Reading for Diversity

1. *Can you identify key passages in the New Testament that have been especially formative for the Christian community to which you belong?* How do these passages or writings relate to the historical, cultural, and social location of your community?

2. *With which New Testament writings are you most familiar?* With which writings are you least familiar? Are there any New Testament writings you avoid? Why?

3. *Have you thought of the New Testament as one book or as a collection of different writings?* Do you agree that Christians have tended to eclipse the diversity in the New Testament? What might be some benefits of embracing diversity? Difficulties?

4. *Do you have a method for reading the Bible?* How do the five guidelines offered here differ from your usual way of reading? Do you feel comfortable trying this way of reading?

Chapter 2: Paul's Gospel Shaping the Christian Life

1. *In what ways does Paul's letter to the Galatians reflect the dynamics of your community?* What passages in Galatians are most familiar to you? How might the message of Galatians challenge your community?

2. *In what ways do you see the work of God as an expression of grace?* In what ways have you experienced the unconditional love of God? In what ways does a relationship with God liberate people from self-recrimination, shame, or guilt? From the expectations and standards of others? How might grace address issues of self esteem?

3. *In what ways would you describe your parish as a place of grace?* Do people readily accept each other as they are? Are you free to share weaknesses and fears with each other? In what ways might a visitor experience acceptance? In what ways does your community include or relate to people who experience rejection from society?

4. *How do you communicate God's grace in your parish?* How might you create opportunities for people to share stories of grace? How might you create the safety to share stories of pain, rejection, and abuse? In addition to the rite of confession and forgiveness, might your parish also consider celebrating a rite that reaffirms God's justification by grace?

5. *In what ways do you live out of an intentional commitment to the inclusiveness of the gospel?* How could your parish develop a style and a strategy to be more diverse and inclusive?

6. *In what ways do you reflect mutuality in relationships among members?* How can a parish honor each person and seek to involve them in community life in significant ways? Are people in your community treated without distinctions? Rich and poor, male and female, educated or uneducated, long-term members and new members, old and young, different racial or ethnic groups? How might a modern parish ensure that no one dominated or excluded others?

7. *In what ways does your parish express the freedom of Paul's gospel of grace?* How do the decisions of the parish reflect the freedom to live life in response to the Spirit? Does your worship provide opportunities for the spontaneous expression of the Spirit?

8. *In what ways do you share Paul's vision of worldwide reconciliation among nations, cultures, races, ethnic groups, genders, and social classes?* Are there opportunities to be agents of peace and reconciliation in the locale of the parish and in the many arenas of the lives of members? Is your parish involved in resolving religious and national conflicts throughout the world? How might it be?

Chapter 3: Mark's Gospel Shaping the Christian Life

1. *In what ways has the Gospel of Mark given support to members of your congregation?* In what ways might it challenge your congregation?

2. *In what circumstances have you shown the courage of your convictions?* In what ways have you had to overcome fear of rejection or loss or embarrassment or suffering in order for you to take a stand? In what ways has fear prevented you from acting as a Christian?

3. *In what ways have you or your community been a servant to each other or to those outside your community?* What are some roles on the "bottom of the ladder" of power and status today in our society that might be models for a life of service? What Christians have you known in public or in private life who modeled the Markan vision?

4. *Do you have a sense of being an alternative community to the cultural values of status, wealth, and power?* Do you support members

of your community as they struggle with issues of status and power in relation to others? To use authority and resources for the benefit of others?

5. *Does your parish have a sense of mission rooted in what God is doing in the world?* Is your "church-vision" for your congregation designed to serve your larger "kingdom-of-God-vision" for the world? Do your members think of themselves as the church when they are active for the kingdom in daily life?

6. *How does your parish carry out a mission to the world?* How much time and resources are spent on maintaining congregational life itself and how much is the congregation organized to serve the neighborhood around it? In what ways is your congregation engaged in the struggle to overcome suffering and oppression in the neighborhood and the world?

7. *What worship would support the discipleship to which Mark calls us?* In what places might your community gather for worship as a means to connect faith and life? Would small-group support be helpful to this ministry? What worship experiences might support people being Christians in the world? Witnessing? Telling stories of courageous Christians? Do you gather in order to be sent back into the world?

8. *In what ways does your community struggle with the conflict between the values of God's wider kingdom and the self-interests of family, work, company, or nation?* How can the parish support people in this struggle?

Chapter 4: Matthew's Gospel Shaping the Christian Life

1. *In what ways does your community reflect the values portrayed by Matthew?* What passages in Matthew are most familiar to you? How have these passages affected your life and commitments? In what ways might the Gospel of Matthew challenge your community?

2. *In what ways have you, in your life and in your community, struggled to be people of integrity?* What are some of the moral dilemmas you have faced? In what ways has God provided guidance and courage to carry out moral decisions?

3. *Have you had times in your life when you became aware of your own hypocrisy?* Has your church been a place to reflect on blindness and hypocrisy? How might it be? Do you think that the church could make use of a version of the Twelve-Step Program

of Alcoholics Anonymous that was adapted for the Christian life in general?

4. *In what ways has your congregation been a place to wrestle with moral issues?* Do you have study groups to discuss church social statements? Retreats where you seek to uncover racism, sexism, and other forms of discrimination?

5. *What is your reaction to the Sermon on the Mount?* Do you experience Jesus' expectations as burdensome or guilt-producing? Have you experienced Jesus' yoke as light and restful? Have you felt empowered by Jesus' blessing and forgiveness and presence?

6. *How might a parish community nurture the reality of God as loving and caring parent?* In what ways does your parish celebrate the goodness of God as a source of inspiration for your life? In what ways is it helpful to relate to God as Father and Mother?

7. *What worship experiences might reflect the Gospel of Matthew?* Might litanies of repentance for personal and corporate sins be helpful? Rituals in which forgiveness is received and celebrated? In what ways does your worship liberate participants from guilt rather than generating it?

8. *Do you see integrity as an issue in society?* How could the church have an impact on society by fostering integrity among its members? By identifying and acknowledging the hypocrisy in the society? In what ways can the church be a light for the world and preserving salt for the earth? In what ways might your parish promote peace-making and lead the nation in feeding the hungry and clothing the naked?

Chapter 5: Luke's Gospel Shaping the Christian Life

1. *In what ways does your community reflect the values expressed in Luke's vision of the kingdom of God?* In what ways might the Gospel of Luke challenge your community?

2. *In what ways have you experienced mercy and compassion in your life?* How have experiences of repentance and forgiveness been transforming for you?

3. *Is your congregation composed of people who are not treated as full members of society?* In what ways have members of your congregation experienced what it means to be oppressed? What do you think the church can learn about God's kingdom from those who are marginalized by society?

4. *In what ways does your parish show justice and compassion*

toward the poor, the oppressed, the downtrodden, the disenfranchised, the sick, and the elderly? Has your parish identified the most vulnerable members of your neighborhood or city? Who would they be? What are the factors that hinder our society from showing more compassion for the poor and downtrodden?

5. *In what ways has your parish struggled to understand the economic, social, racial, and political structures of our society that contribute to inequities and inequalities in United States society?* What resources are available in your larger community to help your parish gain such an understanding?

6. *In what ways does your parish work for the transformation of society?* Has your parish ever affirmed or criticized American society on behalf of the poor? How does your parish or how might your parish deal with advocacy and conflict on behalf of the poor?

7. *What are the expressions of the Spirit in your congregation?* Has your parish experienced charismatic renewal? How do you feel about manifestations of the gifts of the Spirit? Do you encourage people with gifts in various healing ministries? How have these experiences contributed to the diverse expressions of faith in your church?

8. *What worship experiences might reflect the Gospel of Luke?* In what ways does your parish celebrate the power of the Holy Spirit in worship? What expressions of joy and praise characterize your worship? Do you include the sharing of meals as a part of your life together?

9. *In what ways is your vision of God's kingdom different from the way the society presently exists?* In what ways does your parish seek to live the vision of the kingdom of God now?

Chapter 6: John's Gospel Shaping the Christian Life

1. *How familiar are you with the Gospel of John in comparison with the other Gospels?* What passages in John are most familiar to your community? In what ways has John's Gospel been an important part of the traditions of your denomination? Your ethnic community?

2. *What religious experiences have you had?* In what ways are they similar to and different from John's understanding of abundant spiritual life?

3. *In what ways have you thought about the spiritual emptiness of our society today?* The deadening of the human spirit in modern

life, work, and culture? How might an understanding of these problems challenge your parish to a renewed vision and purpose today? What difference does it make to see eternal life as existing in the present?

4. *How would you describe the distinctive spirituality of your denomination? Your ethnic community?* What resources might your parish use to foster prayer, meditation, and a closer relationship with God?

5. *What worship experiences might reflect the Gospel of John?* What images or symbols are meaningful to you and your tradition? How might your parish make greater use of contemporary symbols and images? How might worship involve all the senses as vehicles of God's presence? Would you be willing to wash each others' feet or carry out a similar ritual as an expression of mutual love?

6. *What characterizes love among the members of your community?* In what ways is that love rooted in a common experience of the love of God? What characterizes your church's love for those who are not members?

7. *In what ways is your congregation different from the world?* How does your community differ from other organizations? What difference does it make to have bonds of friendship and unity in Christ?

8. *How might a closer relationship with the rest of nature/creation draw one closer to an experience of God?* How might the physical environment within and around the church building help to evoke an experience of the sacred? What could you do to bring the life of nature into your church space?

Chapter 7: Reading for Renewal

1. *Having studied five different models of biblical Christianity, which one(s) might be your favorite?* Why? Which one(s) might be most challenging to you and to your community? Why?

2. *In what ways might your parish foster an appreciation for the diversity in the New Testament?* How might the study of this diversity be a source of renewal for you?

3. *Can you identify the roots of your own tradition in the biblical writings?* What does your denomination contribute in a special way to the whole Christian church? Do you think your denomi-

nation fosters a diversity of approaches to the Christian life? How might your denomination embrace greater diversity among its congregations and ethnic groups?

4. *What can your community do to foster an atmosphere of mutual appreciation for differences among people in your parish?* How might you create an intentional "community of diversity"?

5. *As a Christian community, do you have a relationship with Christians from other denominations?* How might the experience of yoking or covenanting with one or more parishes be a source of renewal? What might be the benefits? The liabilities? How might you go about establishing such a relationship?

6. *In what ways do you nurture diversity and pluralism in your daily lives?* Do you agree that we Christians should function in our daily lives as agents of reconciliation? What resources do you think we have to bring as Christians to the diversity of our society? How would you articulate this mission of the church?

7. *What issues of diversity have not been dealt with in this book?* How would you address those issues and seek to resolve them?

Epilogue: Reflections on Unity

1. *What ways of fostering unity are most appealing to you? Why?* What experiences have you had in which no sense of unity could be achieved?

2. *What are your reflections on the extent and limits of diversity among Christians?* Within a parish? Within particular denominations? Is the canon an adequate model for the diversity and unity of the church?

3. *What difference does it make to think about unity as a reality given by God?* In what ways might your parish foster a greater experience of unity among yourselves? With other Christians? With all people? With the rest of creation?